The Awakened Ape

A Biohacker's Guide To Evolutionary Fitness, Natural Ecstasy, and Stress-Free Living

By

Jevan Pradas

Copyright/Disclaimer

Table of Contents

INTRODUCTION: A PATH TO BLISS

The happiest people in the world don't wear underwear. If they have clothes at all, it is either a simple sheath that covers their genitals or a cloth they wrap around their bodies in colder climates. They have almost no possessions. They don't eat at restaurants, they don't use smartphones, and they don't watch television. They don't have money. They don't even know what money is. What they have is more valuable -- a sense of serenity and self-confidence that would astound the average person. A joie-de-vivre, an easy laugh, and an absence of stress and worry. They love freely and have a deep sense of oneness with the earth.

They are also the healthiest people in the world. They know little, perhaps nothing, of cancer, heart disease, obesity, depression, Alzheimer's, diabetes, allergies or even poor eyesight. They have never been to a doctor. They are athletic, strong and muscular. They do not gain weight as they age or show signs of dementia. Most remarkable of all, for 95 percent of human history, this is an accurate description of the life of nearly every single human being on earth. Skeptical? It's ok, if I hadn't seen it with my own eyes, I might not have believed any of this either.

How can we most enjoy the brief moment of time we have to be alive? This question first struck me sometime during my formative years when the finiteness of life and the certitude of death became palpable and undeniable. A period of existential crisis took hold, and I became obsessed with finding a solution. I consulted everyone from the ancient Greeks to the most cutting-edge scientists in search of an answer, mixing and matching like an alchemist working on the philosopher's stone. Take two parts psychology and anthropology, toss in a hefty portion of evolutionary biology and sprinkle with a dash of Eastern mysticism. Wash, rinse, repeat, until a dozen years later I emerged with the concoction you now hold in your hands. This final elixir is not at all what I expected to find when I set out on this journey. Many of my recommendations will seem at best odd, and at worse sacrilegious, to minds molded in the technology-driven, consumerist milieu of the modern world. But it is only in embracing our primordial nature that the highest happiness can be found.

Since the dawn of our existence up until the advent of agriculture, we scoured the earth from Africa to the Arctic in search of wild game and fresh fruits and vegetables. Along the way, the forces of natural selection attuned us to our environment in such a remarkable way that our hunter-gatherer ancestors felt a natural unity with their surroundings, leading to a life of robust health and merriment. There are tribes of people alive today, hidden in remote jungles of the Amazon and the sprawling Kalahari desert, who still live in this ancient way and enjoy the fruits of life matched to its genetic potential. Most people in modern society look down upon these tribes as relics of the stone age. How unfortunate that they don't have access to the wonders of technology! Yet scientists who have lived among these "primitives" describe them as the happiest and healthiest people they have ever seen.

I know that this goes against everything you have been taught to believe. I majored in philosophy in college and much to the chagrin of the people unfortunate enough to sit across from me at dinner, I questioned and analyzed everything -- from the color of the apples on the table to the most arcane theories of quantum physics. But it never dawned on me that things like stress, worry, and heart disease were modern illnesses. I took it as a given that as I grew older I would slowly lose my mental faculties, my stressful life would cause my nervous system to degenerate, and I would eventually die from cancer. Then, in graduate school, while writing my master's thesis on the evolutionary psychology of health and happiness, I began poring over the anthropological literature involving hunter-gatherers. What I read blew my mind. I didn't understand how this wasn't already public knowledge. I wanted to run out on the street and grab people by the collar, yelling: "Did you know that hunter-gatherers don't get cavities? They don't even brush their teeth!" It is partly in the interests of not looking like a raving lunatic that I have written this book instead.

Luckily, in the last few years, the ancestral health movement, popularly known as "the paleo diet," has become hugely successful, and people around the world are thinner, stronger and suffer from fewer illnesses and chronic conditions as a result. A smashing success, and for those unfamiliar with the basics of paleo eating I have devoted a chapter to it. But in this craze to get healthier, thinner bodies, people consistently left out what I consider to be the far more important question. Why is it that hunter-gatherers were so happy? Why did they have such great mental health?

The Awakened Ape

It may surprise you to know that psychologists began seriously studying happiness – probably the most important question in all of human existence -- only at the turn of the new millennium. Before that, psychologists focused mainly on treating mental illness, helping a person go from being "sick" to functioning "normally." That's where all the money was; people don't pay for a psychologist when they are simply feeling what Freud called "ordinary human unhappiness". Since the question of how to make the most of this one and only existence we have on earth has been my driving motivation throughout my entire life, I was naturally intrigued by this new development in the field of psychology. I wanted to get my hands dirty. I decided to work in a positive psychology laboratory while pursuing my graduate degree in Mind, Brain and Behavior Research. In the last decade, the field of positive psychology has blossomed, with thousands of journal articles and seemingly as many books published on the subject. The modus operandi for studying happiness has been to sample a group from our society and figure out the psychological, social and economic correlations to well-being. Does money buy happiness? Yes, but only to the extent that one is no longer poor. After that, it doesn't seem to matter much how much money you have. People with lots of close friends tend to be reasonably happy, while those who are neurotic are not. Much of this research has been insightful and overall a great boon to our understanding of the human condition. But when asking the question, "What is it that makes a person as happy as possible?" the field of positive psychology has come up short in six key areas. These are the issues I will seek to address and clarify. They correspond to the six sections of this book.

Let us begin.

The Meaning of Life

How strange a thing it is to be alive! To be caught in this maelstrom of conscious experience, with its varied sensations of pleasure, pain, thought and vision. How different it is to be human beings, rather than the rocks and oceans we share the planet with. How did it come to be so? Why do we feel what we feel? Why do we have the desires, likes and dislikes that we do? The average man is too busy, lost in a world of unfulfilled fantasies to question why he has those dreams in the first place. Only after experiencing genuine heartache do we even pay lip service to these most important ideas.

That people can live their entire lives without actually knowing what it means to be a human being is a great misfortune. For without this philosophical foundation, we are liable to flitter away our short lives embroiled in needless dramas, mired in futile pursuits. This section is about steering you back on course, veering you in the direction of what is truly essential. Lest you worry that I am advocating a life of pure asceticism or self-flagellation, I can assure you I am not. This is a book about pleasure and fun, about health and happiness. Using a thought experiment, I will argue that the attainment of such well-being is the highest purpose to which we humans can aspire.

Unfortunately, there exists a cabal of contemporary psychologists who believe that any deliberate attempt to improve our happiness will only backfire. Trying to be happy, they say, will only remind us of our unhappiness. Even such luminaries as John Stuart Mill, the philosopher famous for espousing the view that pleasure was the greatest moral good, once said: "Those are only happy who have their minds fixed on something other than their own happiness."

I disagree. As a biohacker, I have never understood why otherwise sensible people would adopt these inane views of well-being. Biohacking is the principle that the human body is like a machine, and that if we can figure out how it works, we can improve the way it functions. Happiness is not some nebulous ether, but a biophysical state that operates on the principle of cause and effect. In this way, it is similar to having a healthy heart. No doctor would advise his patient to stop trying to have a healthy heart if he wants to have a healthy heart. And no psychologist should be telling anyone that happiness cannot be improved through direct personal intervention in one's own life. If your attempts to become happier are failing, it is not because it is impossible. It is because you are doing it wrong.

Happy Tribes

Most of the research on the happiest human societies has not been done by psychologists, but by anthropologists. This happened completely by accident. When the field of anthropology exploded in the beginning of the 20th century, scientists had no idea that while traveling to the ends of the earth in search of lost tribes they would inadvertently be discovering the happiest people alive. They went out to study their social customs, their ways of gathering food, the tools they used and their sexual habits. The study of their well-being was only ancillary. Yet anthropologist after anthropologist would come out of the jungle marvelling at how fit, confident and relaxed their subjects were.

The public found this hard to accept. They believed that history was a relentless forward march toward a more elevated culture and a better way of life, culminating in modern European and American society -- the apex of human life. No matter where they live, people around the world have an innate bias to assume that their culture is the best culture, and that everyone else in the world are a bunch of poor saps who have had the misfortune to be born in the wrong time and place.

Unlike you.

Riveted by these stories of hunter-gatherers, I traveled deep inside the Amazon rainforest to see these happy tribes with my own eyes. After two days of canoeing up the river and hiking through a dense thicket of vegetation, stepping over poisonous snakes and hearing the sounds of growling jaguars, I reached a community of hunter-gatherers called the Waorani. I found that the women and children laughed and giggled constantly, while the men were stoic, self-confident and stress-free. The anthropologists had been telling the truth all along.

I have sprinkled tales from my time with the Waorani throughout this book.

The Why of Happiness

From an evolutionary perspective, it is pretty easy to understand why nature makes an orgasm so pleasurable. For our genes to live on in their quest for immortality, they must make copies of themselves. To do this, the genes of the male must escape from the body they currently inhabit and find their way into the body of the female, at which point they bond to form a new person programmed to carry their genes further on to the next generation. This heated, sweaty exchange of seminal fluid, the thing that carries us forwards as a species, would seem an odd and perhaps repulsive pastime no one would indulge in if Mother Nature hadn't designed our brains to release pleasure-inducing hormones in the process. Our genes reward us for doing their bidding by making the behaviors that propagate our genes immensely pleasurable. Sex is easy to understand. But why do we feel love, joy, enthusiasm, serenity? Not all animal species feel these emotions. Most do not. So why do humans experience these emotions? What evolutionary purpose do these emotions serve? And what kind of society would allow us to feel these emotions more frequently?

The flip side of happiness is unhappiness, which results from negative emotions. The evolutionary purpose of fear and anxiety is pretty simple. It's not a good thing for our genes to wind up in the belly of a ravenous beast. So over time we evolved a defense mechanism against large, carnivorous predators that might want to eat us. *Hear tiger. See tiger. Fear tiger. Run away.* But for the vast majority of us today, the most fearful predator we will ever come across is our neighbor's fenced-in German shepherd.

So why do so many of us suffer from chronic stress, anxiety and depression? Why is our stress response on constant alert when we have relatively little to be genuinely worried about? The answer to this will be found in the dramatic mismatch between our current lifestyle and the one in which our genes originally evolved.

Training the Mind

Let's start with exercise. What would it be like if someone from a society where people never exercised a single day in their lives were to meet someone from a society where exercise was built into the very ethos of their community? A society in which, from a very young age, everyone engaged in physical activities like running,

12

jumping, throwing, wrestling and lifting weights. As adults, they would resemble our Olympic athletes.

Now let's say a member of this society -- we will call him Achilles -- was an adventurous type and traveled across the ocean to a distant land where he met the people to whom the very concept of exercise is alien. All the people in this society live a desk-bound existence, and suffer the maladies that result from obesity. How would a conversation between Achilles and a typical denizen of this society go? Something like this: After pulling his boat up onto the shore, Achilles would be met by a dignitary from this roly-poly land named Mr. Rotund.

Mr. Rotund: Well, hello there! (*garbled chewing noises are heard*) Sorry, I was just having a snack (*tosses candy wrapper onto the ground*). Now, then, how do you do? Let me introduce myself. I am Mr. Rotund.

Achilles: Yeah, I can see that. Hi, my name is Achilles, and I have come from far across the sea to find out what kind of people live here.

Mr. Rotund: Achilles! Ah, well that explains it.

Achilles: Explains what?

Mr. Rotund: Why, you are Achilles! You have the muscular body of the Greek gods whose statues stand in our museums. You are only half-human, as your mother was a goddess. That's why you have that incredible physique!

Achilles: Thanks for the comments about my pecs, but that goddess stuff is a silly legend. Let me assure you that I have two fully human parents, and there is nothing "spectacular" about my physique. This is what all humans look like. I, on the other hand, have never seen a creature like you before. You are, not to sound too rude, a bit on the tubby side. In our culture, only the women have protruding mammaries like yours.

Mr. Rotund: Do you mean to tell me that you have no obesity in your society? (*Huffing and puffing as he waddles through the sand.*) That people from your society don't get diabetes or die young from heart attacks? Hold on, let's slow down the pace; I'm getting a bit winded. Now where was I? Oh yes, are you telling me that people in your society don't suffer from hypertension or strokes?

Achilles: Obesity? Diabetes? Stroke? I've never heard of these things. Are those diseases you get due to your immense girth?

Mr. Rotund: Yes! And they are terrible conditions.

Achilles: Mr. Rotund, my friend, I don't understand. Why would you ever let your body get like this?

Returning from our imaginary meeting, let me suggest the following: Achilles, as depicted in our story, could very well have been one of our paleolithic ancestors. Anthropologist Jared Diamond has remarked that the hunter-gatherers he visited have physiques that resemble miniature bodybuilders. And these people don't go to the gym! Their low-fat, muscular physiques result from living and eating the way a "wild" (human) animal is supposed to. They move frequently, walk long distances daily, often while lugging heavy buckets of water or a large antelope leg on their shoulders. Do this every day of your life and you're going to look like an underwear model.

Contemporary life is spent sitting in chairs. As a result of this sedentary lifestyle, we watch our bodies generate excess blubber around our midsections until the once beautiful, strong and powerful apes that we started out as are barely recognizable. Those of us disinclined to turn into pear-shaped piglets use a technique to stimulate muscle growth and improve our cardiovascular system. We call this *exercise*. Modern life is so far removed from the way our bodies are supposed to move naturally that without regular exercise our physical health will rapidly deteriorate.

Now here is the important point -- just as our physical health will decline from the sedentary lifestyle we have adopted in the modern world, our mental health is in equal peril from this unnatural environment we find ourselves in. Stress, depression and anxiety are the emotional equivalents of diabetes, stroke and hypertension. Hunter-gatherers do not get any of these modern diseases, mental or physical.

Unlike Mr. Rotund, we in the modern world live in a society where the benefits of physical exercise and sport were discovered long before the arrival of the computer and car. So, along with a good diet, we have various ways to combat the decline of our physical health.

But what about our mental health? Are there exercises to combat everyday stress and worry? If so, how often do we perform these exercises? Are we mental Mr. Rotunds, unaware that there is a treatment that would prevent us from experiencing these common psychological afflictions? Are we simply resigned to the idea that stress, worry and low self-esteem are inevitable features of the human condition? What would happen if we were to stumble upon a society whose inhabitants were trained from a very early age in the art of mental exercise, who grew to possess such immense mental strength that some of us might be fooled into thinking they were divine? And what if I were to tell you we have already met these mental Achilles'?

One of the many hippies to travel to Tibet in the 1970's was a young Californian by the name of Alan Wallace. Fed up with western culture, but fascinated by Buddhism, he wanted to learn how to meditate at the feet of the greatest masters, so he joined a Himalayan monastery. It was here that his views regarding mental health were turned completely upside down.

The abbot of the monastery was giving a talk to the monks about a common psychological problem for Tibetans. He lamented that people have a tendency to think too highly of themselves while criticizing others. At the end of the talk, Alan stood up and said, "My problem is not that I have too much pride, but that I often think negatively of myself. I often don't like myself and don't think I am very good." The abbot glanced up at Alan with a sweet expression, smiled and said, "No you don't." The abbot didn't believe him. It wasn't possible. He had never heard of someone not liking themselves before.

Similarly, in a meeting between the Dalai Lama and a group of American psychologists in 1990, one of the psychologists brought up the concept of negative self-talk. Since there are no words in Tibetan that translate into low self-esteem and self-loathing, it took quite a long time for the psychologists to convey what they meant. But this wasn't a translation problem. It was a problem of conceptualization. *Self-loathing? People do that?* The Dalai Lama was incredulous. Once the Dalai Lama understood what they were saying, he turned to the Tibetan monks in the room, and after explaining what the psychologists were suggesting, he asked, "How many of you have experienced this low-self esteem, self-contempt or self-loathing?"

Complete silence.

Here was a psychological state of mind so ubiquitous in our culture that everyone experiences it from time to time, if not every single day. Yet the Tibetans, trained since childhood in the art of a mental exercise they call meditation, acted like they were being told about some alien life form. The Dalai Lama turned back to the psychologists and asked a simple question.

"Why would you ever let your mind get like this?"

The Nature of Reality

The final and most esoteric aspect of happiness that is left out of all the positive psychology books is talk about a deeper nature of reality. Philosophers on the other hand, have discussed this subject since the very beginning. The man who coined the term "philosopher," meaning "lover of wisdom" was Pythagoras, who wove his philosophy into a worldview that only members of his secret sect were privy to. Concrete facts about his life are few; what information we do have about him was written down many years after his death and presents him as a nearly divine figure, who emanated a supernatural glow. Did Pythagoras know secrets of the cosmos that have been lost to us today? Perhaps. Unfortunately, we will never know, as his beliefs died with him and his followers millennia ago. What we do know is that his society practiced communalism, had no personal possessions, followed a strict diet, and adhered to an ethical code of honesty, selflessness and mutual friendship. Advice very similar to what you will find in this book. While the wisdom of Pythagoras has been buried beneath the sands of time, the teachings of an even more luminous figure from the ancient world remain. That is, Siddhartha Gautama, more commonly known as the Buddha, which means "the awakened one."

What is it that he woke up to? Buddhist philosophy states that in our everyday lives we are overcome by delusion, which creates attachment and aversion and causes mental stress. By waking up from this delusion, we attain nirvana. Nirvana literally means 'blowing out,' as in a candle flame. It is by blowing out the flames of attachment, aversion, and ignorance that mental stress can be permanently extinguished. The result is a mind that experiences sublime peace.

Does this sound too good to be true? As scientists, we will examine Buddhism from a secular perspective, focusing on the pragmatic teachings related to ending suffering and increasing happiness, while ignoring the dubious religious elements like reincarnation. How does secular Buddhism stack up to the demands of modern science? Is there truly a reality hidden beneath our eyes that would lead to extraordinary well-being if we could only see it? Is nirvana the highest happiness a human can experience? These questions will be the focus of the second half of this book.

Integration

The Buddhist term 'bodhi' is often translated in English as "enlightenment" or "awakening." Bodhi refers to a special kind of knowledge, that of the causal mechanisms that lead to human suffering. Our aim here is the same, to fully understand the causes and conditions that lead to suffering and happiness, all bolstered by the latest revelations in contemporary science. This book seeks to integrate two separate traditions of ancient wisdom with modern science so that we can live the happiest and healthiest lives possible. By learning about the environment in which our Paleolithic ancestors evolved, and how our genetics are still wired to that way of life, we can begin to organize the external conditions (the diet we need to eat, the exercise we need to do, the sunlight we need to get, and the social relationships we need to build and maintain) that will give us the best chance to flourish, both physically and mentally. From there we will add the most successful techniques ever developed by humans to work on the inner conditions (our ability to relax, focus, and experience states of ecstasy and compassion, etc.) of our mental lives -- that of Buddhist soteriology.

This book is also about integrating what we learn into our daily existence in a modern world. Obviously we can't all live like hunter-gatherers in the Amazon or Buddhist monks in the Himalayas; we have jobs, families, responsibilities. Within the pages of this book, you will find tips on how to live in a more natural way while still waking up every weekday morning to brave the congested commute on your way to the office. As you make changes to your diet, begin a meditation practice and stop using shampoo (more about that later), you will gradually notice a sense of calm and mental balance replacing the stressed-out, habitual thought patterns that previously occupied your mind. Your waist will narrow, your sense of vitality will grow, and even things like the common cold will become an increasingly rare occurrence.

I assume that most people will take their practice only this far. That's fine. There's a lot to be said for being happy, calm and healthy. But for those who feel the calling to make the best of their time on earth and reach the highest peaks possible, this book is also a guide that will point you in the right direction. Follow this path and you may find that one day the world around you has become a dancing, playful thing, imbued with a previously unimaginable serenity and bliss.

I. THE MEANING OF LIFE

Democritus

Who Are We?

Here we find ourselves, the collected dust particles of ancient stars. We popped out from the darkness of our mother's womb into the world, equipped with a biological program intent on making a replica of itself in a futile attempt at immortality. We are alive and subject to the twin experiences of pain and pleasure, but none of this was our idea. What shall we do now? How shall we spend our sojourn on this hunk of rock and water as we careen through the Milky Way, before returning to the darkness?

Enjoy the ride, I say.

How have I come to such a conclusion? Let's start at the beginning. To know who we are, we must know where we came from. And it is perhaps true that all of us -- that is you, me, your dog, the Grand Canyon, Jupiter -- evolved from a dot smaller than the head of a pin 13.8 billion years ago. We call this theory the Big Bang, although a more accurate name would be the Big Stretch, since it was a rapid expansion of the very fabric of space-time from that tiny speck to an enormous size in the fraction of a millisecond. Approximately 378,000 years after this event, the universe had cooled down sufficiently to allow the transformation of energy into the particles hydrogen and helium. These particles roved about in giant clouds of dust and gas called a nebula. As the gravitational pull on the dust particles became stronger, the dust collapsed on itself and formed a spinning disk. Out of this spinning disk, the stars were born.

Stars are our ancestors, and just like their progeny, they have life cycles of their own. They are born, grow in size, and grow old before eventually shrinking and fading away. But not all stars. A select few decide that it is better to burn out in spectacular fashion, with an enormous explosion as bright as 100 million suns. It is this latter death of a star that most interests us. For in these supernovae, the process of nuclear fission and nucleo-synthesis creates the heavier elements on the periodic table. These elements are then sent out into space where they form new nebulas containing more elements than just hydrogen and helium. It was out of one of these nebulas that our solar system came to be 4.6 billion years ago.

First, the star was formed that would grow to become our Sun, our giver of heat and light. Beyond the sun was a spinning disc of a dusty mixture. Millions of years would pass as the dust would gather into lumps, and then giant boulders, then small worlds, and eventually the planets. Our earth formed a core, mantle and crust. It would take another half-billion years before the conditions on earth allowed for an atmosphere and oceans. Soon after that, life began.

For almost all of history, living organisms on Planet Earth existed without knowing why. Fish, dinosaurs and saber-tooth tigers roamed the planet in search of food and sex, but never questioned why they did so. Perhaps it was a thoughtful Neanderthal, sitting around the campfire, who was the first to ask: "What are we? Why are we alive?" He may even have made up a myth involving supernatural beings or all-powerful animals. But he didn't have the correct answer.

The Awakened Ape

More than three billion years after life began, a *homo sapiens* named Charles Darwin returned from his voyage to the Galapagos Islands and declared: "We evolved." There had been trillions of life forms before him, and here he was, the very first one to understand why he existed and what it meant to be alive. Some billions of years ago, somewhere in the primordial soup, a molecule developed the ability to replicate itself. This was the beginning of life on earth. That replicator would make copies of itself, but those copies were not always perfect, and there would be mutations that made the next generation of replicators different from the first. Now we have multiple types of replicators, and some replicators are better or worse at replicating themselves. The better replicators survived, and the poor replicators died off. The most advanced replicators, or as we call them today -- genes -- built biological suits of armor to live inside.

"We are survival machines -- robot vehicles blindly programmed to preserve the selfish molecules known as genes," says Richard Dawkins.

An arms race began, and much like the weapons of the Cold War, those earliest replicators built survival machines of increasing complexity and efficiency. In the beginning, those survival machines took the form of eubacteria, archaea and later on, plants and fungi-like mushrooms, which are more closely related to animals than plants. Nearly a billion years ago, the first multi-cellular animal life, in the form of sponges and jellyfish-like creatures, began to dot the Earth's oceans.

Somewhere around this time came the most important moment in the history of life. Astonishingly, it is rarely talked about it. An adaptation came about -- an adaptation that would make life very different from everything that had previously existed. Life developed the ability to feel.

Before this, the act of being alive held no joy, no sorrow, no anything; it was a cold, mechanical process. With the evolution of feeling, life now had a sensual quality. Where exactly this happened and what might constitute a precise definition of "feeling" is a matter of interesting philosophical debate. Did this happen in a single instant? Was there a point in history when no one felt anything at all, and then suddenly, a non-feeling mother gave birth to a creature with the ability to feel? My intuition tells me that the precise definition of "feeling" would need to be deciphered, that there were organisms that sort of could, but sort of couldn't, feel, depending on how you interpreted it. Does a fish feel pain in the way we feel pain? We shall leave that discussion for others. What is important for our purposes is that eons later, we, the descendents of these first "feelers," do experience pain and pleasure.

Why Do We Feel What We Feel?

Our great-great-great (add a million more greats) grandmother was a worm-like creature who lived 550 million years ago. She is important because she is a bilateria, from which the vast majority of all animals today are descendants. Bilateria are animals that have two sides; a left and a right, which are fairly symmetrical to each other as well as a front where the head is, a body cavity that holds the internal organs and an anus that expels waste. Can you think of an animal that doesn't have this anatomical structure?

If you are well-versed in zoology, you may have noticed that I mentioned the answer earlier: the jellyfish. But examples of non-bilateria animals are rare. This adaptation was highly successful and involves a brain at the front of the animal with nerve cords branching out into each of the body parts.

The earliest nervous systems involved the functions of attraction and aversion, in order to move away from harm, and move toward food and mates. At this point, the only things that animals felt were basic sensations such as hot, cold, sexual excitement and hunger. In the beginning, this was mostly a matter of reflex, but somewhere between the arrival of amphibians and that of reptiles, animals evolved the ability to become aware of their sensory pain and pleasure. They began to deliberately seek out pleasurable sensations. The lizard would scamper away from the shade and into the sunlight where it would bask in the warm glow. From that point on, animals would be motivated to seek pleasure and avoid pain, while remaining completely oblivious to the underlying evolutionary reasons they were experiencing these feelings in the first place.

It's fairly easy to understand the benefits of having the ability to experience pain and pleasure. Pain is a punishment for doing something that hinders our evolutionary fitness. Suppose one of our ancestors leapt from a high distance and landed awkwardly on his ankle. If he did not experience pain, he might be tempted to run and jump on it some more, causing himself further damage. By experiencing pain, we learn when to stop and let our bodies recover. By experiencing cold, our bodies tell us that we need to find a warmer spot in the sun. Pleasurable sensations are evolution's way of drawing us toward things that are good for us, and rewarding us when we obtain those things. The delicious taste of a ripe peach is the body's reward for obtaining essential nutrients. The endorphin release during aerobic exercise is the reward for keeping yourself healthy and fit. It should come as no big surprise that an orgasm is so enjoyable because sexual intercourse is a necessary step toward the reproduction of genes.

Mammals, birds and perhaps even honeybees don't simply experience pleasant and unpleasant sensations. They also experience a more complex sensation; we call this emotion. Why did emotions evolve? Once again, we have Charles Darwin to thank for the answer. His 1872 book, *The Expression of Emotion in Man and Animal,* is to this day considered the greatest treatise on the subject of emotion ever written.

Emotions, Darwin argued, are functional. They evolved to serve a purpose; to drive us to perform an action or reward us for a behavior that advanced our evolutionary fitness. The emotions we experience evolved at different times in our history. The most primal emotions, such as fear, are associated with ancient parts of the brain that have been around since pre-mammalian times. The fear response alerts us to danger and kicks the body into flight or fight mode. Our hearts start beating faster; adrenaline rushes through our nervous system, we start taking quick, shallow breaths and blood flows to our large muscles. The function of fear is to urge the body to either run away from a predator trying to make lunch out of us, or to fight for our lives.

Sadness is often felt when we lose something valuable to us. This could be a mate, a child or our social status. The function of sadness is to motivate us to avoid future losses, or to change our living conditions if our current situation is making us feel sad. The physiological and behavioral signs of sadness, marked by slow motor function, fatigue and weeping are also cues to other members of our group that we need aid and comfort.

Is there any reason to experience anger other than to punch someone's lights out? According to a recent evolutionary theory called the recalibration theory of anger, the answer is yes. Anger arises when there is an interpersonal dispute involving a conflict of interests. In any conflict of interests, a calculation must be made to determine how much one should care about one's own personal welfare versus the welfare of others.

Say you are a monkey living in the jungle, and you and your troop are swinging from branch to branch when suddenly you stumble upon a banana tree. Wonderful! You are hungry, and there are enough bananas to feed everyone as long as you share them equally. But before you know it, the monkeys who reached the tree first are gathering up the bananas and taking all the ripe ones for themselves! *"How dare they?!"* you think. *"How could they be so selfish? Everyone deserves a ripe banana!"*

And your blood begins to boil.

Your body has triggered the anger response to prepare you to confront the selfish monkeys of your troop. You might have to fight them for the bananas if they do not listen to reason. Or if they see that you are seething, they may decide that these ripe, delicious bananas are not worth a fight and relent. Thus, your anger has served an evolutionary purpose. You were hungry and needed nourishment. Your body alerted you to the fact that you were being treated unfairly by others and prepared you to deal with the situation. By becoming angry, you let others know that they need to put more emphasis on your own welfare and a bit less on their own.

While the emotions we have discussed are rather unpleasant to experience, the next one we will talk about can be either good or bad, depending on context. Consider the following true story. It is widely known that conjugal passion often begins to fade after a few years. Bill and his wife hadn't been setting the bedroom on fire in quite some time, but Bill had a feeling that today might be different. It was his birthday, and his wife had taken him out to dinner. She was wearing a skimpy dress and acting in an unusually flirtatious fashion, seductively reapplying her rosy red make-up at the table and puffing out her cleavage to make sure Bill got a good view. To top it all off, she excused herself to the bathroom at one point and came back, reaching under the table and handing Bill her panties.

Returning home, Bill's wife told him to go wait in the basement where they had an entertainment room and giant television. Meanwhile, she would go upstairs to slip into something more comfortable. Things were definitely looking up for Bill. Literally looking up. He was sure that tonight was the night that months of sexual frustration would come to an end. Excited, he decided to speed up the process, and as soon as his wife was out of sight he began to undress. He chucked his clothes into the hallway closet and opened the door to the basement, galloping down the stairs.

"SURPRISE!"

The look of horror shared by Bill and the 30 friends that had gathered in the basement for a surprise party was, well, horrific. The shock sent Bill tumbling right down the stairs, frantically trying to cover his throbbing manhood, while simultaneously making sure not to crack his skull on the rock-hard basement floor.

The emotion of surprise quickly alerts us to something in the environment that demands our immediate attention. In the grip of surprise, our eyes widen to take in more of the visual field, and our attention, which just moments earlier could have been scattered all over the place, becomes highly focused. In this sense, surprise is closely related to fear, but without the negative connotation. Had Bill descended the stairs with his clothes on, the surprise would have been a happy one. Are you getting all this, Bill?

The function of negative emotions is easy to explain; the evolutionary value of positive emotions is a bit more difficult to assess. Recently, biologists and evolutionary psychologists have made some headway in explaining how positive emotions promote certain adaptive behaviors.

While a negative emotion is an adaptive response to a perceived threat, positive emotions are fitness-enhancing responses to perceived opportunities. As opposed to solitary creatures like sharks, human beings are a social species that depend on the help of others to survive and raise children. It is essential to have physiological feedback that rewards pro-social behavior. Feel-good emotions such as compassion, joy and happiness evolved in order to facilitate social interactions between people, and to cement bonds. By rewarding us with these positive emotions, Mother Nature has given human beings an incentive to form and maintain relationships with other human beings, increasing our chances of surviving and replicating.

Other positive emotions, like pride, are meant to augment our social standing. Imagine that you have just won a wrestling tournament or received an award at work. You feel a sense of pride, you walk with a little strut in your step. In place of your normally slumped shoulders, you stick out your chest and stand a bit taller. Think of colloquial sayings encouraging someone who is feeling down to buck up: "Hold your head high," "Keep your chin up." Standing tall with one's chest puffed out and one's chin up is a display of dominance in the primate world, and is perceived by others as an indicator of high status.

Imagine that after a long, hard day of manual labor out in the sun, you kick back on your porch with a cold brew and some good food as you rock back and forth in your beloved rocking chair. Ah, contentment! This is the evolutionary reward for satiating your basic needs; or, in the words of positive psychologist Barbara Frederickson, the opportunity to "savor and integrate" your recent successes.

But what of the strongest emotion of all: the one that can start a war, the light of your life, the fire in your loins. Throughout history, human beings have tried to impart a divine origin to the emotion of love, but make no mistake, love, just like all the other emotions, is an evolutionary adaptation designed to solve the problem of reproduction. There are many kinds of love, love being a catch-all phrase for different types of feeling. Maternal love is different from brotherly love. Romantic love is entirely different from the love one feels for one's children. But each type of love evolved to address a specific problem.

The Giant Panda has no need for romantic love, as the female panda is only fertile for two or three weeks of the year. During this time, a few males will compete for her affections, the dominant male getting to mount her several times before returning to his solitary life of lounging about and gnawing on bamboo. Human females are different. They are fertile throughout the year; the times when they are ovulating are generally hidden from males; and couples will usually mate for many months before producing children. According to the famed evolutionary psychologist David Buss, we evolved an emotion needed to solve the problem of commitment. How can I be certain my partner will ignore all these other suitors and stick around long enough to get pregnant and have children? How do I know she won't just dump me the next time someone slightly more appealing rolls around?

Enter romantic love, the biological drug meant to intoxicate you in the presence of another person. When you are in love, you spend your days obsessing over the other person. Constantly intruding daydreams make work, social obligations, or just about anything else all but impossible. You idolize her, you think every little thing she does is perfection itself. It makes it hard to concentrate on paperwork.

As well it should. Your genes have a plan for you, and that plan involves the rendezvous of semen and egg and the nurturing of that tiny fetus into a person of its own. And to do this your genes are going to make you a bit irrational, at least for a while. That irrationality will be just about the most powerful and pleasant experience you will ever have. And when those kids come along, the intense bond of parental love will be needed to motivate you to hang around and raise your offspring, unlike snakes and iguanas. If not for love, why else would you spend so much of your time caring for that crying, screaming, needy, totally ungrateful little monster? Nature, it is said, deliberately made babies adorable. Otherwise, their parents would strangle them.

Coming full circle, it is conscious creatures like us who have evolved according to the laws of natural selection. We are the "survival machines" of all those genes inside us, diligently doing their bidding so that they may replicate themselves in the next generation. They reward us with pleasant feelings for perceived opportunity and success while flooding our system with negativity if we deviate from the prescribed path. It is this ability to feel -- to either enjoy life or fall into a deep depression -- that gives human life meaning.

Hedonism

We are heading into philosophical territory, a source of great pleasure to many, a headache to others. Do not fear a little exercise for your brain, my companions, for the unexamined life is not worth living. Of course, you are free to ignore Socrates' advice and spend the rest of your days in the frivolous pursuits a gang of marketing mavens designed for you. Or you can spend a few minutes thinking about what's truly important. What should be the goal of your life? What does it mean to have lived well? Heavy questions, yes, but hey, you only live once. Seems like a worthwhile endeavor, don't you think? So relax, settle back in your recliner, and kick off your shoes. I'm here to espouse hedonism, good, old-fashioned hedonism. Just a different version of hedonism than you might expect.

When the average person hears the word "hedonism," he thinks about sex, drugs and chocolate cake, maybe all at the same time. But in the philosophical world, the doctrine of hedonism states that pleasure is the only intrinsic good, and pain the only intrinsic bad. By "intrinsic" we mean something that is valuable for its own sake, as opposed to something that is only valuable if it is used to acquire something else that is intrinsically valuable. Pleasure is considered an intrinsic good, because even if the joy you felt led to no other benefit, the experience itself would still be a positive one. Money, on the other hand is an example of an item that is "instrumentally" valuable . Money can be used to acquire goods that can lead to positive states of mind; merely the knowledge that one has money can bring about peace of mind. But even the largest stack of green paper is not in itself valuable.

For the ethical hedonist, the goal of life should be to maximize pleasure and minimize pain. Pleasure is not limited to fleeting joys, such as the high from a drug, or intense, profoundly diverting but otherwise meaningless sex. It can also be the deep and loving bond a mother feels for her child, or anything else that feels good. Nor is pain simply the feeling of stubbing your toe; it can also take the form of stress, nervousness, jealousy, anxiety, boredom, the sound of a shrill laugh. Hedonist philosophers have been around since the beginning of recorded history. In the *Epic of Gilgamesh,* the character Sudari says: "Fill your belly. Day and night make merry. Let days be full of joy. Dance and make music day and night... These things alone are the concern of men."

Not everyone is convinced that hedonism is a good thing. In fact, I can already hear that skeptic inside your brain protesting.

Skeptic: I agree that happiness is important in life. But at the end of my life when I am lying on my deathbed, what I really want is to look back at all the amazing experiences I've had. The trips I took, the family I raised, the adventures I had, regardless of whether or not I felt happy at the time.

Answer (abbreviated simply as "A" from now on): Here is my countervaling thought experiment. I call it "The Case of the Highly Accomplished Anhedonist." *Anhedonia* is a real-life psychological condition where, due to an abnormality in the brain, people are unable to experience pleasure from activities that most people find enjoyable. Socializing, exercising, listening to music, even an orgasm brings them no joy.

Now, imagine that you suffer from anhedonia. But unlike real-life anhedonists, you happen to be wildly successful in all the domains our society normally honors and even envies. Having won the genetic lottery, your dashing looks grace the cover of high-class fashion magazines, and members of the opposite sex throw themselves at you like moths to a flame. Your intelligence and solid work ethic have allowed you to go to Harvard, where you made connections with other creative and brilliant people, and together you started a company you subsequently sold for billions of dollars. With more money than you could possibly spend in your lifetime, and all the free time you could ever want, you decide to travel the world, having all sorts of adventures.

But when you lie on the beach in Thailand, you feel no pleasant sensation from the warm sun on your skin, no refreshing coolness as the ocean water laps over your legs. When you hike up Mount Kilimanjaro and gaze out over the vast African plains, you experience no awe, no feeling of wonder, no sense of accomplishment despite completing an exhausting challenge.

You marry a beautiful partner who, despite your inability to feel sensual pleasure, cares for you deeply. But you feel no love, no excitement, no passion as you lie there in her warm embrace. When you fool around in bed at night you experience no sexual pleasure. You are only going through the motions. Not even the climax excites you. Years later, you experience no delight as your child takes her first steps or says her first word.

Decades pass, and eventually you succumb to serious illness and lay on your deathbed. You look back on your life and review all that you have accomplished. You are successful beyond anybody's wildest dreams, yet you enjoyed none of it. Even now there is no sense of satisfaction from a life well lived. The question I put to you is: Would *you* want this life?

Of course you wouldn't. You would not feel love, happiness, enjoyment or any of the hedonistic pleasures that make life worth living. What this shows is that what we consider life's "successes" are not ends in themselves. Being rich, good-looking, and getting to travel to far-off places and have wonderful friends are not valuable in their own right; they are only valuable because of the pleasurable feelings these things give us. There is no point in reaching the summit of the highest mountain if you can't enjoy the view from the top. There would be no point in becoming an olympic-class skier if you got no rush from racing down a slope.

What gives value to anything in life is the effect it has on the quality of experience of conscious creatures. Nothing else really matters. Nothing else has intrinsic value. And since we prefer pleasurable experiences to painful ones, we might as well devote ourselves to maximizing the feelings we enjoy versus the feelings we don't, not just in ourselves, but in the world around us. If everyone had this goal, the world would be a pretty great place to live.

How Do We Find Out How to Enjoy Life?

Skeptic: All right, you've convinced me! Time to open up the Bordeaux! I'm going to lean back and put my feet up. *Calls out to wife in another room:* "Darling, I've decided to become a hedonist. I'm sipping a nice glass of wine by the fire, nibbling on brie, and listening to Moonlight Sonata. To make things absolutely perfect, I'm going to need you to come in here and give me a foot massage!"

Wife calls back: "Yeah, fat chance, buddy! Time to take out the garbage."

Skeptic: You know, maybe this hedonism thing isn't going to work out. Maybe, those psychologists who say that chasing after happiness will only lead to unhappiness were right.

A: If you spend your life chasing sensual pleasures or avoiding any activity that frightens you, those psychologists are definitely right: That won't make you happy. Better to take the advice of Democritus, the ancient Greek philosopher most famous for originating the theory that the universe consisted of atoms. His contemporaries called him the laughing philosopher, because he advocated living a cheerful life. While it is true that he loved the occasional drunken bacchanal, he thought that the most pleasure came from a serene, internal state of mind, a pleasant disposition that one carefully cultivated.

You too can cultivate such a disposition.

We will do this by taking a systems-thinking approach to the human body, called biohacking. We are biological machines, and there is no reason we can't hack nature's design and reconfigure it to make us feel spectacular. Professional athletes already do this for sport. They are continually searching for an advantage by studying the science of exercise physiology, biomechanics, and the art of injecting illicit chemical compounds into their rear ends. They use this knowledge to train their bodies to reach peak performance. If we can break down the mechanics of the human body to improve athletic performance, why can't we do the same for our well-being? Once we understand the how and why of happiness, we can take our cue from these athletes, train our minds, and achieve optimal well-being.

Evolutionary Fitness and Happiness

Evolutionary fitness is our ability to pass on our genes, taking into account both natural and sexual selection. These genes developed a signal, a sense of well-being, to reward our ancestors for behaving in ways that led to evolutionary fitness. But the genes also punished our ancestors with stress signals when they were acting in ways harmful to the genes' ability to self-replicate. To figure out how to achieve well-being, we need to know exactly what our genes like and don't like. The problem is the environment we live in today, is different from the environment in which these signals originally evolved. Our signals are all out of whack. To solve the riddle of human happiness, we have to study the people who live in this ancient way. What we'll find, will cause you to re-evaluate everything you thought you knew about health and happiness.

II. HAPPY TRIBES

Pygmies

Of all the mysteries of Africa, none is more fascinating than the saga of the nation of tiny people who live hidden away deep within its dense rainforests. The earliest record of their existence comes from the correspondence of the eight-year-old Egyptian Pharaoh Pepe II (throne name Neferkare) around 2250 B.C.E.. After receiving word from Harkhuf, one of his governors, that amongst the bounteous treasures found in their expeditions to the South was a dancing dwarf, the young Pharaoh could hardly contain his excitement. He writes:

I have noted your letter, which you have sent in order that the King might know that you descended in safety from Yam with the army which was with you. You have said in this letter that you have brought a dancing dwarf of the god from the land of spirits...

Come northward to the court immediately; you shall bring this dwarf with you, which thou bringest living and healthy from the land of spirits, for the dances of the god, to gladden the heart of the King of Upper and Lower Egypt, Neferkare, who lives forever. When he goes down with you into the vessel, appoint excellent people, who shall be beside him on each side of the vessel; take care lest he fall into the water. When he sleeps at night appoint excellent people, who shall sleep beside him in his tent. My majesty desires to see this dwarf more than the gifts of Sinai and Punt. If thou arrivest at court with this dwarf being alive, prosperous and healthy, my majesty will do for thee a greater thing than which was done for the treasurer of the god Burded in the time of Isis, according to the heart's desire of my majesty to see the dwarf.

Outside of Africa, stories of these tiny people gained a mythical status. In the *Illiad*, Homer writes of cranes who fly south during the winter to attack and kill Pygmy nations. Where Homer got the idea that Pygmies engaged in life or death battle with large, murderous birds is a mystery, but the story was widespread. Pottery dating back to 424 B.C.E shows Pygmies in mortal combat with these giant cranes. The great philosopher Aristotle, a bit more skeptical perhaps, omitted the crane-Pygmy war in his book *History of Animals:* "The storks pass from the plains of Scythia to the marsh of upper Egypt, towards the sources of the Nile. This is the district in which the pygmies inhabit, whose existence is not a fable. There really is, as men say a species of men of little stature, and their horses are little also. They pass their life in caverns."

But a few centuries later, the famous Greek historian Pliny the Elder favored Homer's view of the Pygmies.

Beyond these in the most outlying mountain region we are told of the Three-Span Pygmae who do not exceed three spans, that is, twenty-seven inches, in height; the climate is healthy and always spring-like, as it is protected on the north by a range of mountains; this tribe Homer has also recorded as being at war with cranes. It is reported that in springtime their entire band, mounted on the backs of rams and she-goats armed with arrows, goes in a body down to the sea and eats the cranes' eggs and chickens, and that this outing occupies three months; and that otherwise they could not protect themselves against the flocks of cranes [who] would grow up;

and that their houses are made of mud and feathers and egg-shell.

Clearly, the ancient world suffered from a shortage of reliable testimony regarding the lives of these mysterious Pygmies. But early attempts at gathering empirical evidence often proved fatal. An Arab slave trader from the 1st-century B.C.E by the name of Abed Bin Juma became entranced by the stories he heard of these dwarf people. He marched his caravan through the treacherous jungles of present-day Zaire in hopes of encountering the Pygmies. When he finally found them, he reported being "fiercely received by the malicious little demons who sprang from the soil like mushrooms, and showered their poisoned arrows on the travelers."

Nearly two thousand years later the mythical status of the Pygmies had hardly diminished. The early European explorers of Africa were told incredible stories by non-Pygmy African tribes of dwarf people with tails who were excellent elephant hunters due to their extraordinary power to make themselves invisible. When the white man and the Pygmies finally did meet, the previous hostility exhibited by the Pygmies toward outsiders proved justified. The explorers treated the Pygmies like animals. The early 19th century explorers captured the Pygmy children and transported them to zoos all across Europe. Even the United States participated in these horrific acts. In 1906, the Bronx Zoo placed a Pygmy from the Mbuti tribe named Ota Benga in the monkey house, along with the other primates. He shot his bows and arrows, and showed off his pointed teeth (filed into sharp fangs, as was the custom in his tribe) to adoring crowds. People came by the thousands to see him. The newspapers reported that he would get into wild wrestling matches with an orangutan, and establish dominion over the other primates, speaking to them in his native guttural tongue, which they seemed to understand.

Anthropologists have since come a long way in their understanding of Pygmies, who are now defined as an ethnic group in which the height of adult males is on average less than 4 feet 11 inches tall. And while they may not have the magical powers once ascribed to them, the story I will tell of the Pygmies is no less astonishing than the tall (or should I say short) tales told to outsiders of the Pygmy people. For the Pygmies hold the answer to the greatest question ever posed by mankind: the secret of how to find happiness.

Many different groups of Pygmies exist today, with as many as a half-million living in the central African rainforest. When John Lennon wrote "Imagine," he might easily have been describing traditional African Pygmy society. The Pygmies have few possessions, and no one is described as either rich or poor. They pay no taxes, have no laws, and everything is shared. Polygamous and monogamous behavior are both accepted. They work half as much as we do and have an abundance of leisure time. Pygmies don't slave away all day at dreary, repetitive jobs to raise cash to buy more stuff they don't need. Pygmies do something a tad more thrilling than navigating a shopping cart through a supermarket aisle. They hunt wild animals, using nets, spears, bows and arrows. Small prey, like the tiny forest antelope, run too quickly to chase after on foot, so the Pygmies surround the antelope and flush it out, eventually catching it with a net before pouncing on it and quickly killing it. Every once in a while, the Pygmies will hunt much larger and more dangerous game. Elephants.

To hunt an elephant, the Pygmy will track the elephant's large tracks through the jungle. He will paint his face black so that if he is spotted by his prey, the elephant will think he is a monkey. The Pygmy will sneak up on the elephant and jam a spear into its belly, then turn around and sprint back through the forest. The elephant will slowly bleed to death. The Pygmy merely has to follow the increasingly bloody trail until the elephant eventually collapses.

Upon the death of the elephant, a great feast is held, and neighboring tribes from all around the region will gather to celebrate. Festivities include dancing, singing and love-making, as people rejoice because the forest has provided them with enough meat to last a long time. Anthropologist Kevin Duffy spent time living with the Mtubi Pygmies, and it is to his excellent work *Children of the Forest* that I am most indebted. This is how he describes a day in the life of the Pygmies:

What do the Mbuti do when they don't have to hunt and gather? Plenty. But first there are always the routine chores that make a camp function: collecting firewood, fetching water, cooking the morning meal, and tending the children. Yet with the sheer exuberance and joy of living that I have seen only among the Mbuti, there were also spontaneous dances and singing, adding to the sounds of a happy camp. At the forest's edge laughing children were swinging from a hanging vine a hundred feet long while nearby girls were acrobatically skipping rope, using a length of a liana with the greatest dexterity.

Compared to the practices of the Pygmies, sex in the 21st century seems downright puritanical. The Pygmies' amorous adventures begin at an early age. The moment they hit puberty, the Mbuti begin to engage in daily sex with many different members of the tribe. This period of free love lasts for a year or so before they get married and start having children.

Strangest of all is the courtship Duffy himself engaged in with a Pygmy woman named Alita. She was the smallest girl in the camp, standing under four feet tall. Alita also had a problem; she was related to everyone else in the camp. While sleeping with cousins is all good fun, and the Pygmies consider it a natural part of growing up, a Pygmy is forbidden to marry a relative. This left our 5'10", white anthropologist as the only available bachelor living in the camp. And Alita had her eyes on him.

Alita's cousin Sukali acted as matchmaker. He led Duffy to a river stream where Alita and Sukali's wife were bathing naked. When they arrived, Sukali grabbed his wife and they ran into the forest for some spontaneous lovemaking, leaving Duffy and Alita alone. Perhaps he can be forgiven for not being around any normal-sized women in a while, but I still find his attraction for the yardstick-high Alita very curious, especially the glowing terms in which he describes their flirtation, a tit-for-tat that he was apparently losing. As he writes:

"I was beginning to feel that I had lost command of the situation to this tiny-girl woman, this miniature Venus who had risen lovely and flowerlike from the spring with drops of water glistening on the petals of her golden body."

Deciding to be a gentleman, at least for the moment, he did not sleep with this aboriginal Thumbelina right then. Instead they walked back to camp, but not before running into Sukali and his wife having sex on the mossy floor. They paid little notice to Duffy, even though he nearly stumbled over them. Ever the dutiful anthropologist, Duffy noted to himself that the Pygmies were not copulating in the missionary position.

Later that night, during a torrential downpour, Duffy was alone in his hut when the tiny, muddy-footed Alita came in to sleep with him. After teasing us with a chapter of lightweight erotica, Duffy skips over the best part, leaving out the juicy details. How in the world did he physically have sex with a three-foot tall Pygmy girl? How did she feel about sleeping with a giant? What position were they in when the deed was done? What was their pillow talk like? These are things the anthropological record simply demands.

More than their *laissez-faire* attitude towards sex and their intriguing way of obtaining food, the Pygmies have a zest for life, which is always bubbling up to the surface and can explode into song and dance at any moment. This *joie de vivre* can be attributed to their oneness with their natural environment and their lack of concern for the future or interest in the past. The Pygmies are as well-adapted to their environment as any other species that resides in the forest with them. Their way of life has never driven a single species of plant or animal into extinction. They look upon the forest as their parent and consider themselves the children of the forest. The forest is a sacred place, much like a mosque or a temple, except that *this* holy land is a living, breathing entity, filled with exotic wildlife. Underneath the canopy of tall trees reside majestic, rarely seen animals like the Okapi, an eight foot-tall relative of the giraffe, with a beautiful dark brown coat covering it's midsection and black and white zebra stripes running down its legs. In the land of the Pygmy, giant hogs and colorful peacocks co-exist with boisterous chimpanzees. The sounds of the forest range from a peaceful silence to the howling of monkeys to a cacophony of songs from birds and crickets.

In the Ituri Forest, where most Pygmies live, the temperature rarely drops below 72 degrees and humidity is usually 100 percent. The only clothing the Pygmies wear is a G-string woven from tree fibers. No one is self-conscious about being naked. For shelter, they build small huts out of nearby sticks and leaves. These huts look like green igloos, with only a tiny opening one crawls through to enter. Pygmies do not worry about what will happen to them in the weeks, months and years to come, as they trust that the forest will provide all that they need to live, just as the forest always has. Duffy writes:

To the Mbuti, the past is unimportant because it is gone completely and forever. As for the future, they have little desire to control what does not yet exist. The present is something that happens every day, and is to be enjoyed with consideration for others, with love, and sometimes with passion. The Mbuti's natural and total harmony with their ecosystem is something from which all people can learn...and we should remember them well, for the Mbuti mirror our past. They are the living spirits of our not-so-distant hunting-and-gathering ancestors.

Anthropologist Colin Turnball agrees. He says "the [Mbuti pygmies] were a people who had found in the forest something that made their life more than just worth living, something that made it, with all its hardships and problems and tragedies, a wonderful thing full of joy and happiness and free of care."

Echoing these statements, anthropologist Paul Schebesta writes of the same Pygmies:

The pygmies stand before us as one of the most natural of human races, as people who live exclusively in compliance with nature and without violation of their physical organism. Among their principal traits are an unusually sturdy naturalness and liveliness, and an unparalleled cheerfulness and freedom from care. They are people whose lives pass in compliance with the laws of nature.

47

The mystery of the Pygmy people continues into the new century. Scientists still debate the cause of their short stature. Some believe their diminutive size allows them to be nimble and quick as they scamper through the dense rainforests. Recent theories suggest that their small height can be attributed to their shorter life spans. Pygmies rarely live much longer than 40 years, but this is not necessarily due to their harsh environment or some illness, but rather to the speed with which they reach reproductive age. Pygmy children develop much quicker than normal children and by the age of two are already expert archers, who can hunt small game within a year or two. Pygmy girls start taking care of younger children by age six. In fact, Pygmy children and normal children grow at about the same rate, but the Pygmy will stop growing by the age of 12, having reached his full height of around four feet. By the age of 20, a Pygmy woman will have already had several children and will appear middle-aged.

A great tragedy has overcome many of the African Pygmies in recent years, as their hunter-gatherer way of life has been menaced. Today, many are forced to work as slave laborers for their taller neighbors. Yet in other parts of the world, their mythology continues to grow. In March, 2013, rangers from the Way Kambas national park in Indonesia claimed to have spotted dozens of naked Pygmies no more than 20 inches tall, sporting dreadlocks down to their waist. Do these miniature people really exist in the dense forest of the park? While the enigma of the Pygmies continues to baffle us, what we do know is that their hunter-gatherer lifestyle and their intimate bond with their natural surroundings has led them to a happiness unknown to modern society.

New World Savages

Some time ago, perhaps 15,000 years in the past, the *megafauna* (also known as the comically large animals) of Siberia decided that they had had more than enough of that desolate place, and chose to make a break for greener pastures. When you are a human being living in Siberia, and your survival depends on eating woolly mammoths and mastodons, and these gigantic elephant-like creatures suddenly decide that they want to get out of Dodge, you have little choice but to pick up your spear and follow them. This is how the first Paleo-Indians came to occupy the Great North American continent. They followed these enormous beasts across a land-and-ice bridge that once connected Siberia and Alaska. This area is now known as the Bering Strait.

The nomads then followed the newly opened coastline (thanks to the vanishing ice age), and headed south and eventually east. These regions, uninhabited by people, abounded with bison and other wild game, and in a relatively short period of time, millions of humans were flourishing in North and South America.

Thousands of years later, explorers from a far-off land would cross the ocean and pay them a visit. These sailors came from a culture that had been practicing agriculture and living in large cities for over 10,000 years. They had completely forgotten the old, natural way of life that humans had pursued since the dawn of man. It is this collision between such vastly different societies, in a world still filled with mystery and wonder, that so fascinates us.

Every American child knows the story of Christopher Columbus sailing with the *Nina*, the *Pinta* and the *Santa Maria* from the shores of Spain to the Caribbean. As adults, we learn that Columbus was a profoundly flawed human being. But few of us ever hear the story of the beautiful people Columbus stumbled upon on those isles.

Columbus describes the natives he met in the first letter that he wrote about his voyage:

The inhabitants of both sexes of this and of all the other islands I have seen, or of which I have any knowledge, always go as naked as they came into the world, except that some of the women cover their private parts with leaves or branches, or a veil of cotton, which they prepare themselves for this purpose... [their bodies] are well made...they are very guileless and honest, and very liberal of all they have. No one refuses the asker anything that he possesses; on the contrary they themselves invite us to ask for it. They manifest the greatest affection towards all of us, exchanging valuable things for trifles, content with the very least thing or nothing at all...They are neither lazy nor awkward; but, on the contrary, are of an excellent and acute understanding. Those who have sailed these seas give excellent accounts of everything; but they have never seen men wearing clothes, or ships like ours.

Columbus said that he had to put a stop to the unfair trading his sailors engaged in. In his eyes, trading iron nails for large pieces of gold was unjust. Of course, in the very next paragraph Columbus boasts that with 50 men he could subjugate the entire island and bring back as many servants and slaves as the King desired. A complex man, Columbus.

The Spanish subjugation of the Caribbean natives in the name of gold, God and glory in the years to come was horrifying. Needing gold to pay back the money invested in their expeditions, the Spaniards enslaved the Indians and forced them to work in mines. When no gold was found, the Spaniards took their Indians slaves back to Europe. They killed without conscience or mercy; the conquistadors even tested out the sharpness of their swords by slicing up innocent Indians. It was genocide. A fascinating and brutal history, but one I shall pass over, as it takes us away from our main concern: the lives of these supposedly "primitive" Indians before the Spanish conquest.

For that, we gain more insight from Amerigo Vespucci, who reputedly traveled on four expeditions to South America a few years after Columbus. Whether he went on the first and fourth voyages is widely disputed, but the middle two definitely happened. On his "second" voyage, Vespucci writes that upon seeing the Spanish ships for the first time, the South American natives jumped into their canoes and paddled out to meet them. But the Spaniards had other plans. They wanted to take them captive. So when the canoes got close enough, they bore down on the natives with their ship in hopes of capsizing the canoes and taking them prisoner. The natives abandoned their canoes and swam six miles safely to shore. Vespucci noted that the Indians were far faster runners and much better swimmers than the Christians.

When the Europeans reached the mainland, they spent about three weeks exploring and were altogether friendly with the natives they found. Curious natives came every day from farther inland to marvel at their boats and white skin. Leaving the mainland, the Europeans set sail to explore other parts of the new world, reaching a small island off the coast. On this island, they found human footprints of colossal size. Anxious to see what sort of people could possibly have such large feet, they trekked off into the valley, eventually coming upon some huts. There they found two old women and three young girls. All of them were enormous. Vespucci, for whom the American continents are named, says: "The children were of such lofty stature that, for the wonder of the thing, we wanted to keep them." The Europeans planned to kidnap the frightened, abnormally tall young girls and bring them back to Castille. Their plans were foiled when "as many as thirty-six men, much bigger than the women, and so well made that it was a rare thing to behold them" showed up, brandishing spears. Vespucci and his companions decided to saunter back out of the village and make their way back to the ships. Acting as if nothing had happened.

In a 1502 letter attributed to him, describing his "third" voyage, Vespucci tells much more about the natives and their way of life:

We found the region inhabited by a race of people who were entirely naked, both men and women... They have large, square-built bodies, and well proportioned. Their color reddish, which I think is caused by their going naked and exposed to the sun. Their hair is plentiful and black. They are agile in walking, and of quick sight. They are of a free and good-looking expression of countenance. They have no laws, and no religious belief, but live according to the dictates of nature alone. They know nothing of the immortality of the soul; they have no private property, but every thing in common; they have no boundaries of kingdom or province, they obey no king or lord, for it is wholly unnecessary, as they have no laws, and each one is his own master.

So far, so good. But then things take a rather strange turn. After describing the odd facial piercing habits of the natives, Vespucci says:

The women, as I have said, go naked, and are very libidinous, yet their bodies are comely; but they are as wild as can be imagined... They make the penis of their husbands swell to such a size as to appear deformed; and this is accomplished by a certain artifice, being the bite of some poisonous animal, and by reason of this many lose their virile organ and remain eunuchs.

Clearly primitive life was not superior to the modern version in all ways. As much as I enjoy the company of seductive, resourceful women, I am quite content with modern foreplay bereft of venomous creatures. Vespucci also wrote that the natives rarely got sick, lived to be 150 years old, and were surprised that Europeans didn't eat their enemies, given that the taste of human flesh is quite excellent.

Despite Vespucci's obvious exaggerations, the news of the natives cannibalism spread throughout Europe, and the populace soon thought of them as savages. These were creatures who ran around naked, lived without law and order, and ceremoniously ate the corpses of those they had bested in war. Brutal savages they must be! The great 16th century philosopher, Michel De Montaigne, became fascinated by the discoveries being made in the new world. He spent time with the explorers, and interviewed the Brazilian natives they brought back to France. He found them to be just as perplexed by European society as the Europeans were perplexed by theirs. They could not understand for instance, why such large, armed and bearded men (the King's guard) would allow themselves to be bossed around by a child (the 13-year old King Charles IX), or more poignantly, how there could be such a large disparity of wealth between those with castles and servants and all sorts of riches, while outside their doors were beggars, emaciated and hungry. Montaigne came to a more enlightened conclusion regarding their "barbarism". In his essay "Of Cannibals," he writes:

These nations seem to me, then, barbaric in that they have been little refashioned by the human mind and are still quite close to their original simplicity. They are still ruled by natural laws, only slightly corrupted by ours. They are in such a state of purity that I am sometimes saddened by the thought that we did not discover them earlier, when there were people who would have known how to judge them better than we. It displeases me that Lycurgus or Plato didn't know them, for it seems to me that these peoples surpass not only the portraits which poetry has made of the Golden Age and all the invented, imaginary notions of the ideal state of humanity, but even the conceptions and the very aims of philosophers themselves. They could not imagine such a pure and simple nature as we encounter in them; nor would they have been able to believe that our society might be maintained with so little artifice and social structure.

This is a people, I would say to Plato, among whom there is no commerce at all, no knowledge of letters, no knowledge of numbers, nor any judges, or political superiority, no habit of service, riches, or poverty, no contracts, no inheritance, no divisions of property, no occupations but easy ones, no respect for any relationship except ordinary family ones, no clothes, no agriculture, no metal, no use of wine or wheat. The very words which mean "lie," "treason," "deception," "greed," "envy," "slander" and "forgiveness" are unknown. How far his imaginary Republic would be from such perfection.

Benjamin Franklin was a wise and intelligent man who admired the natives of the new world. He wrote about the extraordinary quality of life, nobility and civility of these people, still commonly referred to by his countrymen as "savages." The Indians were generally seen by the North American settlers – most of them hard-working Protestants -- as being poor, ignorant and uneducated. The Indians had a different view. Franklin writes: "Having few artificial wants, they have abundance of leisure for improvement by conversation. Our laborious manner of life compared with theirs, they esteem slavish and base; and the learning on which we value ourselves, they regard as frivolous and useless."

Franklin goes on to tell a story about how the state of Virginia thought it would be a great benefit to the Indians to set up a college fund, so that six kids from neighboring tribes could attend a college in Williamsburg. The Indians thought it over for a day and came back with a polite reply. First, they profusely thanked the government of Virginia for making such a kind offer, knowing that the government had the interests of the Indians in mind, and no doubt believed that the kind of learning taught in their colleges was of great value. But, this experiment had been tried before, with Indian children going off to school to learn the knowledge of the white man and then returning to the Indian tribes completely useless, saying that "They were bad runners, ignorant of every means of living in the woods...could not withstand the heat or cold, knew nothing of how to hunt or build a cabin...spoke our language imperfectly...they were totally good for nothing."

Franklin had other things to say about the happiness and tranquility of Indian life. He couldn't help noticing that while Indians seemed disinclined to ditch their culture for the Euro-American one, many Euro-Americans were more than willing to become Indians. Franklin supplied this example. He had heard of a person who had been captured by the Indians, lived with them for a few years and was later rescued by his own people. He returned home to a sizable estate. Wealthy, free from care, back among friends, this man would surely want to remain in civilized society, right? Wrong. Before long he grew tired of the effort needed to maintain such a lifestyle, turned his estate over to his younger brother and, taking only a rifle and a matchcoat, "took his way again to the Wilderness." Franklin used this story to illustrate his point that, "no European who has tasted Savage Life can afterwards bear to live in our societies." Such societies, wrote Franklin, provided their members with greater opportunities for happiness than European cultures.

Cannibals of the South Pacific

Starving, freezing from a torrential downpour, and lost in the jungle of a tropical island in the middle of the Pacific Ocean, Herman Melville saw his first sign of human life in many days: a well-beaten path leading to a remote village of tiki huts and loincloth-wearing natives. Of the two main tribes that inhabited that island there were the Happar, known for being friendly and cordial; and the Typee, by reputation cannibals who would feast on the American's white flesh if given the chance. There was no way of knowing which of the tribes this path led to. While the idea of ending up as someone's dinner wasn't an appealing prospect, Melville, weak and shivering, had no chance of surviving in the jungle without help. Better to take a 50/50 chance at staying alive than a slow and painful death at the hands of Mother Nature. He stepped onto the path.

The path led to the Typee village.

Today Herman Melville is best known as the author of the literary classic *Moby-Dick*. During his life, however, he was known as the man who lived among the cannibals. The tale of his time spent with these savages offers a glimpse into daily human life before the intrusion of the modern world.

Melville was filled with *wanderlust* and had an independent streak from a very young age. Wishing to be free of family support and determined to make a life for himself that included adventure and traveling, the 20-year-old Melville signed up to be a crew member on the *Acushnet*, a whaling ship that would go on a journey through the Pacific Ocean. Eighteen months later, sick of the long trip and the unfair treatment he thought the workers received, Melville decided to jump ship while it was docked in the Marquesas Islands of the South Pacific.

He and a fellow shipmate made a daring escape from the boat and headed for the hills. Overly confident in their ability to survive in the jungle, they found harsh reality encroaching on them after only a few days. Starving and without reliable shelter to protect themselves from the heavy rain, they knew that weren't going to survive on their own. They needed to seek refuge amongst the island's natives. And so they staggered on to that dirt trail, not knowing what awaited them.

Miraculously, they were received by the locals with open arms. The pair was given food to eat, a thatched roof to sleep under and even a "personal assistant." A man named Kory Kory helped Herman adjust to the strange but leisurely life in the valley. One of Kory Kory's duties was to carry Melville -- who had injured his leg during his escape -- through the jungle on his back wherever he went. In fact, Melville was treated so well that he worried that the Typee might be fattening him up for the kill.

"Not to worry," they told him. He would not be eaten; that was a fate reserved for the wicked members of the Happar tribe during times of war.

Melville would spend three weeks living among the Typee before leaving the valley to return to the seafaring life on another whaling ship. While he may have taken a few liberties in turning his adventure into the semi-autobiographical *Typee* -- the work for which he was best known during his lifetime -- there can be little doubt that his description of the Typee people and their way of life is accurate. His account is corroborated by his shipmate as being truthful. What's more, his descriptions of the natives match those supplied by other explorers who had visited the Marquesas Islands.

Melville described the average day in the life of the Typee this way: "Nothing can be more uniform and undiversified than the life of the Typees; one tranquil day of ease and happiness follows another in quiet succession." The Typee were not early risers, but awoke well after sunrise. First, they'd head down to the stream and bathe in the cool waters, breathing in the fresh air, frolicking about for 30 minutes or so before heading back to the house for breakfast, which was a light affair consisting of fruit and coconuts. The residents of the house would sit around on the mats and engage in cheerful conversation as they ate. After this, pipes were lit and passed around, though each person took only a few puffs.

From there people went their own way. Some would go back to sleep; others would head out into the groves to collect fruit or bark fibers. Some of the girls would spend time adorning themselves with flowers and lathering their bodies with oils. Men could use this time to sharpen their spears or carve wooden designs. After the morning's light work, the afternoon was a time for a glorious siesta in which everyone partook. This usually lasted about an hour-and-a-half; then came another round of pipe smoking, before preparations for the largest meal of the day. Melville would often eat his afternoon lunch with the rest of the bachelors in a place called the "Ti" which was reserved for men only, the primordial version of a men's club. There, he dined on roasted pork. "The Ti was a right jovial place," he tells us. "It did my heart well, as well as my body, good to visit it. Secure from female intrusion, there was no restraint upon the hilarity of the warriors, who, like gentlemen of Europe after the cloth is drawn and the ladies retire, freely indulged their mirth."

As evening approached Melville would take a canoe out on the lake with a pretty young girl or bathe in the stream with the others. When the sun went down, torches were lit and the natives began chanting and storytelling. "All sorts of social festivities served to while away the time," Melville writes. "The young girls very often danced by the moonlight in front of their dwellings."

Finally, everyone would retire to the house where they slept, or dozed for a bit, before waking to eat the final meal of the day, and then pass around the tobacco pipe one more time before collapsing into a deep sleep. "The Native strength of their constitution is in no way shown more emphatically than in the quantity of sleep they can endure," he tells us. "To many of them, indeed, life is little else than an often interrupted and luxurious nap."

Maasai

Joseph Lekuton is not your average Harvard graduate. Long before he strolled through those vaunted Ivy League corridors, he was known as Lemasolai, meaning "proud one," a name given to him by an elder member of his Maasai tribe, a group of nomadic cow herders who roam the African Savannah.

At the age of 14, Lemasolai was coming into his own, and he, along with his brother and a couple of friends were tasked with getting the cows fed and kept away from ticks. They walked 24 miles in a single day to take their cattle herd down to the lowlands where there was bright green grass to eat. Upon reaching this fertile land, they set up camp, built a fire, drank themselves full with milk and told stories about the girls they liked. Now with the fire nearly out, Lemasolai spread his cowhide on the bare soil, closed his eyes and dozed off peacefully under the canopy of stars.

He would open them again to the sound of rainfall in the middle of the night. Strange, he thought, it had been a perfectly clear night when he went to sleep, and while it was cloudy now there was only a faint hint of a drizzle. No, the sound he was hearing was not rain. The cows were peeing, all of them. There is only one thing that can make cows this frightened.

Lions.

The Awakened Ape

He got up, eyes still trying to adjust to the pitch black night. The sound of a roaring lion shattered the night air. Chaos ensued, the cows started running, blindly bumping into each other and Lemosolai as well. He could barely see, and was armed only with a small club, useless against the most ferocious predator in all of Africa. Yet he and his friends heard the menacing roar and ran towards the lion. Cows are the lifeblood of the Maasai tribe, so they must be saved at all cost. But the wheezing sound of desperation coming from a cow being taken by the throat signaled to them that it was already too late. The lions had their kill.

On this night, the lions proved too clever. Two lions had attacked the cattle herd, but not together. One had circled around to the south side of the camp, where Lemosalai and his friends were sleeping, while the other lion lay in wait north of the camp. With the wind blowing from south to north, the smell of the southern lion frightened the cows, and they stampeded north -- right into the paws of the waiting beast. It was an ambush; the cows never had a chance.

The next day Lemosolai and his friends knew what had to be done. They would have to track down the lions and kill them. Otherwise, the lions would keep attacking the herd. When they awoke, they set out to find the marauding beasts, which proved easy. The lions were devouring the cow no more than a hundred yards from where the boys had slept. As they approached, the female lion got up and wandered off. But the male lion, not yet sated and face still buried inside the cow, stayed. He didn't want to give up his kill; he was going to stand his ground. The giant male roared. Lemosolai could feel his heart thumping through his chest. The lion got up, covered in blood and started pacing back and forth, roaring loudly, and studying the feet of the Maasai teenagers to see which one was going to attack first.

It wasn't going to be Lemosolai. This was too dangerous for him. So he gave his spear to his older brother and ran towards the nearest cattle camp to get more help. But just as he left he saw that the warriors from the nearest camp were already on their way and when the lion saw the men coming, he dashed off.

When the boys returned to the main camp, his friends told everyone that he had been scared of the lion. He was mocked incessantly. "Oh look, there's Lemasolai! He's the one who is scared of lions. What a coward!" The same way a boy in the United States might be mocked for being scared of harmless daddy long-leg spiders.

To the Maasai, cows are special animals. They provide the tribe with everything they need. The Maasai have longed baffled nutritionists with their diet, consisting of (in order of amount of consumption) raw milk, raw blood and raw meat. Some Maasai villages eat a small amount of fruits and vegetables as well, though many villages do not eat any fruits or vegetables at all.

If you believe standard nutritional advice, you'd think this high-fat diet would be deadly. But the Maasai suffer from almost no diseases. They don't get dental caries, they don't have high blood pressure, heart disease is almost unheard of. And despite consuming an astonishing, one might even argue insane, amount of cholesterol, their cholesterol levels are half that of the average American.

Unfortunately for the Maasai, in recent years the regional government has pressured them into a more pastoral way of life. The Maasai have added grains, especially corn maize, to their diet. This has resulted in poorer health, though they are still healthier than people living in the West.

The Awakened Ape

Despite the government's meddling, the Maasai have largely been able to maintain their traditional ways. They live in huts made from sticks, mud, and dung. They do not have paying jobs. Instead, they herd their cattle and live as nomads. Like the Pygmies, the Maasai are famous for their height, but for the opposite reason. The Maasai are among the tallest people on earth, with lean and slender physiques. The Maasai also happen to be one of the few tribal communities whose happiness has been quantified by researchers. The results are astonishing.

Asked to rate how satisfied they were with their lives -- on a scale of 1 to 7 -- the average Maasai rated himself a 6.4. Fair enough. But the researchers didn't stop there. They wanted to get a feel for the emotions the Maasai experienced throughout the day. Were they more likely to experience positive emotions such as joy, affection and contentment, or negative emotions such as sadness, anger, guilt and worry? The researchers created a scale called the Perfect Happiness Scale. This measure ranged from -100 to +100. A score of 0 meant one experienced equal amounts of positive and negative emotions, and a score of 100 meant perfect happiness (the highest degree of positive emotions possible with no negative emotions). The mean score for the Maasai was a 70, with 100 percent of the 127 tribe members logging a score above neutral. Not only that, but a large portion of the members claimed to have never experienced sadness or guilt. And a few claimed to have never experienced any negative emotions at all.

I was so blown away when I read this study that I had to see how their happiness stacked up against a modern sample. Using a data set from a study of happiness I was conducting at San Francisco State University, I compared the Maasai to a contemporary group of Americans and Western Europeans. After translating the data onto the

Perfect Happiness Scale, I found the mean score of my modern population to be 22/100, with 69 percent of the participants reporting "above neutral." If being happy is taken to mean experiencing more positive than negative emotions, then yes, more people today are happy than are unhappy. But among the Maasai studied, literally everyone was happy. The average Maasai was more than three times happier than modern Westerners. In fact, only six percent of the people in my study scored as high on the Perfect Happiness scale as the average Maasai.

The natural way of life is so powerful, that despite having to face voracious lions and undergo ritualistic teenage genital mutilation (both boys and girls), their happiness reigns supreme over ours.

Piraha

Daniel Everett was living with the Piraha tribesman of the Amazon rainforest when a tempestuous storm came through and blew over the houses in the village. The Piraha sat and watched as their homes turned from beautiful dwellings into scattered debris, laughing the whole time. When they finished laughing, they got up and started building new homes.

"The Piraha laugh about everything," Everett writes in his book *Don't Sleep; There are Snakes*. He adds:

They laugh when they catch a lot of fish. They laugh when they catch no fish. They laugh when they're full and they laugh when they're hungry. When they are sober, they are never demanding or rude. Since my first night among them I have been impressed with their patience, their happiness, and their kindness. This pervasive happiness is hard to explain, though I believe that the Pirahãs are so confident and secure in their ability to handle anything that their environment throws at them that they can enjoy whatever comes their way. This is not at all because their lives are easy, but because they are good at what they do.

As a teenager, Everett was selling LSD outside a Jimi Hendrix concert when he met a cute girl who happened to be the daughter of missionaries. And so began his conversion to a deeply religious brand of Christianity. He ended up going to Bible college and decided that he wanted to become a missionary himself. He yearned to bring the Lord's message to people in remote parts of the world. He yearned to be their savior. And that's how he ended up far away from modern civilization in the heart of the Amazon.

The task of converting the Piraha to Christianity was daunting. Many had tried and failed. Everett spent years studying, planning. First, he had to learn Portuguese so that when he got to Brazil he could talk to the locals and get them to take him to where the Piraha lived, deep within the exotic Amazon rainforest. The tribe had very little contact with the outside world and spoke their own language. A language that no one else in the world knew how to speak. So Everett also had to learn linguistic techniques that would help him to learn a language that resembled nothing he had ever heard before. When the day he met the tribe finally came, he had to hope that they would accept him and allow him to live with them, even though he had no way to verbally communicate with them.

When he got there, his first impression was that the Piraha lived like a bunch of hippies on a campout. They seemed to spend most of their time laying around, relaxing. By his reckoning, they only worked about 15 hours a week. Now, it is common for preconceptions to cloud our judgment, and Dan had gone into the Amazon with the idea that the Piraha were primitive people. But he soon came to see that the Piraha were extraordinarily adept in all the ways necessary to survive in their environment. The Piraha, he reports, can walk into the jungle "naked, with no tools or weapons, and walk out three days later with a basket of fruits, nuts and small game." Every man, woman and child has detailed knowledge about the plants and animals that live near them. They are hunter-gatherers and eat a wide variety of foods and always have enough. They do not show concern about where their next meal will come from, as they have the ability to go out and get food whenever they want. They are exceptionally good fishermen, and especially adept with a bow and arrow. Everett claims that they rarely miss a target. If they are using a bow and arrow to fish, and three arrows go into the water, three dead fish come out. All this he found quite remarkable.

Years passed, Everett biding his time. After living with the tribe for so long, he had gained their trust and learned their language. All the hard planning and work of the last decade led up to this moment. It was time to tell them the story of Jesus Christ. It was time to save their souls.

Powerful sermons meant to convert nonbelievers have a certain structure. You're supposed to talk about your own weaknesses, about how Christianity saved you, about how you once were blind but now you could see. Everett told them a story about his stepmother's suicide. This was supposed to trigger a powerful emotional response. But after telling this story, he was greeted by laughter. He was hurt and confused. "What's so funny? Why are you laughing?" he asked.

"You people kill yourselves?" the Piraha replied. "We don't do that. What is this?" It was not that they were mean-spirited or had a cruel sense of humor; it was the very notion of suicide that struck them as unbelievably bizarre and outrageous. And then it dawned on Everett! He had come here to save the Piraha, but they weren't the ones who needed saving. He writes:

I realized they don't have a word for worry, they don't have any concept of depression, they don't have any schizophrenia or a lot of the mental health problems, and they treat people very well. If someone does have any sort of handicap, and the only ones I'm aware of are physical, they take very good care of them. When people get old, they feed them.

Still, Everett was determined that his training should not go to waste. He was a true believer; he thought he was doing good by telling them how Jesus would want them to live. So while living with the Piraha, every once in a while, he would pepper them with inspiring anecdotes about Jesus, explaining Christian theology and morality, hoping that the Piraha would change their ways.

One morning, he was sitting around drinking coffee when one of the Piraha said: "Dan, I want to talk with you. We like you, we know you live with us because the land is beautiful, and we have plenty of fish, and you don't have that in the United States...but you know we have had people come and tell us about Jesus before. Somebody else told us about Jesus, and then the other guy came and told us about Jesus, and now you're telling us about Jesus, and we really like you but, see, we're not Americans, and we don't want to know about Jesus. We like to drink, and we like to have a good time, and we like, you know...to have sex with many people, both women and men. So don't tell us anymore about Jesus or God. We are tired of it." And then they ate him.

Just kidding.

Having failed with this group, Dan picked up his stuff and moved to another Piraha village. After spending some years with them, Dan once again tried to deliver his pitch. This time, he at least got the Piraha to ask a few questions about Jesus. "What color was this Jesus? Was he white like you or brown like us? And how tall was he? Did he like to hunt and fish?"

"Well, I don't know," said Dan. "I never saw him."

"You never saw him? Your dad saw him, then?"

"No, he didn't see him, either."

"Then who saw him? Someone must have seen him."

"Well, they are all dead, it was a long time ago."

"Then why are you telling us about this guy? If you never saw him and you don't know anyone who ever saw him?"

With that conversation, Everett began to have a change of heart. The Piraha were radical empiricists who wouldn't believe anything without evidence in front of their very eyes. The concept of God, as often as he tried to explain it, was completely foreign to them, and they could not be made to understand it. They were peaceful and happy. He thought about using some of the more deceitful missionary tactics that had been deployed in other parts of the world where tribal people lived happily. To get people to accept the Gospel, you first had to destroy their culture by introducing capitalism. Create a desire in them for material goods, and tribal people would go from being content with what they had to seeing themselves as poor and stranded at the bottom of the totem pole. It's when people suffer that they are most open to being saved.

But Dan couldn't do that. He realized that his attempts at changing their culture would end up ruining something rare, precious and beautiful. The Piraha lived without a feeling of guilt; they had no concept of sin; they rarely got angry. He also was struck by the Piraha's skeptical attitude towards anything they didn't have direct knowledge of. He began to doubt his own beliefs, eventually giving them up altogether and becoming an atheist. He had gone to the Amazon to convert the Piraha. In the end the Piraha converted him.

The Piraha have fascinated researchers for other reasons as well, causing a bit of a stir in the field of linguistics. The way they phrase sentences goes against well-established theories previously thought to be air-tight. They also have no concept of numbers. Not even the number one. Despite many attempts over an eight-month period to teach them basic concepts of math that any toddler could understand, Everett found that with the Piraha, it was a case of in one ear and out the other. Usually, the lessons ended up with the Piraha rolling around the floor shrieking with laughter.

The Piraha have no creation myths. They rarely talk about the past or make plans for the future. They live in the here-and-now. The only thing that matters to them is what is happening in the present. And of course, they are extremely happy. A team of psychologists from MIT went down to the Amazon to study the Piraha and remarked that they were the happiest people they had ever seen. As one of them explained, "I have not looked at them for any one period of time and not seen the majority of them happy."

The Happiness of Tribal Societies

Far removed from modern industrial society hunter-gatherers, hunter-horticulturists and other traditional societies have been pushed to the edges of the earth. They no longer live and hunt on the most fertile grounds, and few of these societies still exist without at least some awareness of a modern world just beyond their borders. Despite such problems, these people offer us the best glimpse of what life was like for much of human history. How do we know this? These societies are scattered across the globe, from the Amazon rainforest to the deserts of Africa, yet they have remarkably similar social organization. Anthropologists assume that when we find universal human traits today, these are traits that were present in our common ancestors. When combined with archeological evidence, we have compelling reasons to believe that the essential organization of these tribal societies has remained relatively stable for tens of thousands of years. Oblivious to most types of agriculture and ignorant of modern technology, these people live off the land in a way we shall consider "natural" and "wild."

The question is: Are they happy?

I have already spoken about the pastoralist Maasai tribe experiencing far more emotions that are positive than are negative, at a ratio well above what would be considered "flourishing" in the United States. Furthermore, 98 percent of those sampled said that they were satisfied with their lives. In a more limited study concerning well-being, the hunter-gatherer !Kung Bushmen of Northern Botswana were found to have "relative freedom from mental stress." The Kaluli people living in the dangerous highlands of Papua New Guinea are equally remarkable. Over 2,000 members were extensively studied for signs of mental illness over a 10-year span and during that time there was only one case of a person displaying marginal depressive symptoms.

There exists an abundance of qualitative data on the well-being of these traditional societies to support these empirical studies. Anthropologists who have spent time with these assorted peoples indicate that the members of the tribes are quite happy. After visiting the Maasai and the Hadza, evolutionary biologist Bjorne Grinde said that they "probably enjoyed a superior quality of life" to people living in contemporary society. Dr. Weston Price traveled all over the world studying "primitive" societies, marveling at the physical and mental well-being of these supposedly backwards people. Discussing the Polynesian Islanders, he remarked, "The characteristics of the Polynesian race included straight hair, oval features, happy, buoyant dispositions and splendid physiques." Speaking of the Torres Straight Islanders, he wrote:

It would be difficult to find a more happy and contented people than the primitives in the Torres Strait Islands as they lived without contact with modern civilization. Indeed, they seem to resent very acutely the modern intrusion. They not only have perfect bodies, but an associated personality and character with a high degree of excellence. One is continually impressed with happiness, peace and health while in their congenial presence.

Of the forest Indians who live in the north of Canada, he says, "I have seldom, if ever seen such happy people as the Forest Indians of the Far North." Meanwhile, the people of the Marquesas Islands were:

Enthusiastically extolled for their beauty and excellence of physical development by the early navigators...They reported the Marquesans as vivacious, happy people...The early navigators were so impressed with the beauty and health of these people that they reported the Marquesas Islands as the Garden of Eden.

Anthropologist Verrier Elwin studied the Naga people of the Himalayas. The Naga are mountain folk who wear animal skins, hunt wild game and collect fruits and roots for food. He described them as "Excellent people...strong and self-sufficient with the free and independent appearance of mountain people everywhere...friendly and cheerful, with a good sense of humor, talented, with splendid dances and a love of singing."

Psychotherapist Jean Liedloff spent two-and-a-half years living with Indian tribes of the Amazon. The first group she stayed with, the Taurpin Indians, were the "happiest people I had seen anywhere." That is until she came across another tribe known as the Yequana, who experienced a sense of well-being far beyond what she had ever found in "civilized" society. Perhaps even more extraordinary were the mental states Liedloff noted in the shamans of the Sanema Indians:

The proportion of Sanema who have attained truly impressive states of and harmony with their surroundings is remarkable and would, I am quite certain, be impossible to match anywhere in the West or East. In every clan there are

several who live as lightly and happily as the most advanced
gurus. I know families in which almost every adult member
enjoys these qualities so very rare in civilization.

What is going on here? Why do people who have been
denied the comforts of modern society enjoy a lifestyle that
provides more happiness than those in wealthy, highly
developed industrial societies? And what does this tell us
about human happiness? To unravel this mystery, we need
to understand what I call The Beautiful Truth.

The Beautiful Truth

A female Tasmanian devil will give birth to a litter of 50 children, who once born will scramble to grab one of her four available breasts to suck on. Those who miss out will die. After weaning, the surviving devils will venture out on their own, to live the majority of their lives in seclusion. They will only meet up with other members of their species long enough to fight over food. If it's breeding season, the males will go toe-to-toe for the right to impregnate the females. Come across a devil in the wild and there is a good chance you will find battle scars marking its body. A devil doesn't need to make alliances, build community morale, or care for others. Its emotional needs are to hunt, fight and copulate, three reasons these marsupials are so notoriously irascible. Without any need for the help of others to survive past infancy, a devil has little use for empathy, compassion, joy or love.

But we got lucky. We evolved to experience all of those pleasant emotions. It's not just that we are capable of being happy some of the time. The evidence from studying tribal societies tells us that feeling good is the default setting for wild humans. This is a far cry from the dystopian reality of human life that Thomas Hobbes proposed. He claimed that man, left to a state of nature, would lead a life that was nasty, brutish and short. He could not have been more wrong. The beautiful truth of the human condition is that if our genes are given the proper environment to express themselves, they will reward us with a positive mood.

Why do we experience this happiness, unlike the choleric Tasmanian devil? Primarily, because we are a social species, and as a social species we need to spend time around other people. Otherwise, we won't survive. A day in the life in our ancestral past brimmed with lively social activities -- hunting, gathering, collecting firewood, building huts and strengthening bonds by singing and dancing. It was a lifestyle that required us to have energy, joy and enthusiasm.

Skeptic: Oh, come on. Isn't this just that old noble savage nonsense? What about all the downsides to life in pre-history? Have you forgotten about those? Do you know what an intestinal parasite is?

A: The hunter-gatherer environment is far from Shangri-La. There are infectious diseases and the dangers of the natural world must be dealt with. In the jungle, getting eaten by a jaguar is a clear and present danger. A member of the Kichwa tribe in the Amazon told me that one day he was trying to show off to some tourists by catching a poisonous equis snake by the tail. Talking in the third-person, he told the group, "Watch Fausto distract the snake by waving his left hand, while grabbing it by the tail with his right." The snake ignored his waving left hand, lunged out and bit him on the right hand.

"Are you ok?" the tourists asked him. He assured them that he was fine, walked a bit, and then fainted. The tourists took him to a hospital where he remained for 15 days.

"Primitive" people still have accidents; one of the leading causes of death for jungle-dwelling tribes is death by tree. Either the tree falls on top of you while you are sleeping, or you fall out of the tree while you are trying to collect some delicious honey. In the Polynesian Islands, it is not uncommon to die from a coconut bouncing off your head.

To get injured in hunter-gatherer society is a serious affair. When your livelihood depends on your athletic ability to hunt and gather, a debilitating injury is not something that simply keeps you on the sidelines at rec league basketball for six months. It is a life changer. Even a broken bone might mean that you would become permanently maimed.

Skeptic: Jevan, you're a man of science. What about all the silly beliefs and superstitions these people hold? Isn't there an Amazonian tribe that thinks lobsters are divine?

A: Yes, but sometimes that sort of thing can work in your favor. When I asked a member of the Waorani about the majestic pink river dolphins that make their home in the local waters, I was told that the Waorani hunt those too. "You eat dolphins?" I queried. "Yes" he responded. "And if you kill one, you take its teeth and wear it as a necklace. To do so means you will have lots of girlfriends. My father has such a necklace, and he has two wives. They are sisters."

Of course, when the Waorani first made contact with the outside world, such magic amulets were of no use. The Waorani quickly succumbed to the diseases of the first-world. Not having any knowledge of germs and pathogens, they blamed these illnesses on the curses of neighboring shamans. This led to a series of wars and revenge killings.

Skeptic: Exactly. So what about the violence back then? I've read that their murder rates are far greater than what we see today in modern society.

A: In the Amazon, I stayed at the home of an elderly Kichwa tribe member, whose age was a great mystery, not only to us, but to himself. He may have been the most affable, friendly old person I have ever met. He was constantly laughing and joking around. He taught me how to turn cocoa into chocolate, fixed me a local fermented drink called chicha, and sang songs as we sipped it around a campfire. When it was time for him to go to bed in his shack across the river, he said the hell with taking the canoe, stripped naked and waded across, giggling the whole time. And when he was younger, he killed a bunch of Waorani.

The Waorani, for their part, are famous for the ease at which they kill. The Kichwa refer to them as savages and these two tribes have fought each other throughout history. But the Waorani don't just fight with the Kichwa, they fight with everyone. They killed the first missionary who tried to convert them, they fight with the oil companies, they are currently at war with a nearby tribe called the Taromenane, and they fight with each other.

As I ate with the Waorani, they regaled me with stories of raids, kidnapping, murder and even genocide. A Waorani woman, most likely in her eighties, told me that when she was young her community lived as nomads and slept in the trees in order to avoid other Waorani groups. And yet, when I asked her if life was better before contact with the modern world, she gave me an unequivocal yes. They were very happy back then. The moral of this story: We might just have to accept the paradox that people can be killers and yet still be happy.

The Awakened Ape

Actually, whether ancient hunter-gatherers were more prone to killing than modern society is a hotly debated topic. Some scientists look at a tribe like the Waorani and take this as evidence that our ancestors also lived in a similar state of violence. Other anthropologists retort that if there is violence among contemporary tribes it is only because they have been pushed to remote corners of the globe where they have to compete for limited resources. But if you look at tribes like the Hadza, who have no natural enemies and a relatively large space to operate in, you don't see this warfare. Our ancestors would have had the whole world to exploit and hence no need to fight over resources. Anthropologists point to evidence that our hunter-gatherer (abbreviated as HG from now on) ancestors lived peacefully and experienced far less violence than neolithic peoples.

Skeptic: War, gut-eating worms, poisonous snakes, and no cardiologists? No way, Jose. I don't want to live like them!

A: The hunter-gatherer lifestyle, in the past or today, is not utopian. But it is their happiness in spite of all the dangers they face that is most remarkable. If they lived in an utopian paradise, their serenity could easily be explained. Instead, HG's are a testament to how naturally strong and resilient human beings are supposed to be. It's a way of life that has bewildered Westerners who have gone to live with them. National Geographic writer Michael Finkel tells of a leading member of the Hadza tribe named Onwas:

Onwas, as he repeatedly told me, doesn't worry about the future. He doesn't worry about anything. No Hadza I met, in fact, seemed prone to worry. It was a mindset that astounded me, for the Hadza, to my way of thinking, have very legitimate worries. Will I eat tomorrow? Will something eat me tomorrow? Yet they live a remarkably present-tense existence.

Skeptic: Wow! I've got to admit, not worrying sounds pretty good. Still, I've heard stories about HG's getting angry, having fights, crying and grieving. It wasn't just fun and games back in the day.

A: When talking about HG's it's always helpful to exercise a bit of common sense. HG's were still human. Spouses bickered, wives nagged, husbands were unfaithful. People had different temperaments, and you were going to get along better with some members of the group than others. Not all hunter-gatherer tribes were exactly alike either. In the next few chapters, when I describe the various lifestyles of these people, I will be generalizing. If you search hard enough, you could easily find counter-examples of tribes that behave differently. But it's largely irrelevant, because we are after the behavioral and environmental commonalities that the majority of our ancestors became adapted to, and can't waste time on every little exception to the norm. The norm being fit, confident, autonomous and free.

Skeptic: I still don't get it! How can someone not know where their next meal is coming from and still be happy? How can a mother who knows that half her children will die before they reach adulthood be worry-free?

A: To put it succinctly, everything you have been told about happiness is wrong. Happiness is not something that should have to be pursued. Happiness is our birthright. To get stressed out, anxious and fat, we have to muck it up.

And of course, we have. Royally. It is not just our generation's fault. If we want to assign blame, we can go back to around 10,000 years ago when the first people decided to abandon their nomadic ways and settle down to a life of agriculture. While it is true that this change brought with it a certain stability, the growth of large-scale societies and a tidal wave of technological advances brought about such a radical change in our environment that our Stone Age DNA couldn't adapt fast enough. Today, we are cavemen dressed up in a suit and tie. We're lost in a masquerade.

And our genes don't like it.

III. THE WHY OF HAPPINESS

Stress and Discords

A member of the Waorani tribe named Fabiano told me of a time he was casually walking to the outhouse in the middle of the night, when a large black panther leapt out from behind a bush. Fabiano took off, sprinting towards the outhouse door, with the giant cat right on his heels. He ducked inside and slammed the door behind him as the panther's claws scratched against the wood. For the next few hours he sat silently on the toilet as the panther paced back and forth waiting for him to come out. Finally, as the sun rose, the cat gave up and disappeared into the jungle.

Hunter-gathers experience far less stress than we do. How can this be? They get attacked by wild beasts on the way to the pisser. Well, through millions of years of evolution, the human body adapted remarkably well to the type of threats HG's faced. That is: Acute stressors. As Dr. Robert Sapolsky puts it: "Stress on the Savannah was three minutes of intense running and then it was over. Or you were over."

To deal with these situations, our body turns on the fight-or-flight response and galvanizes resources to give energy to where it is most needed: the exercising muscles. The side-effect of this efficiency is that when we put all our energy into the systems of the body that help us to escape danger, our body is neglecting all the systems that are essential to functioning throughout the rest of our life. When we are simply relaxing, our body is quietly engaged in maintenance procedures. Routine stuff like the growth and repair of tissues, immune system functioning, reproduction. During a stressor, our body diverts energy away from these long-term projects into the more immediate bodily functions that help us avoid getting our liver ripped out.

This is fine if we only have to deal with an acute stressor. Once the panther left, Fabiano's heart rate would return to normal, his immune system would start functioning properly, and he would continue to be relaxed until the next time he came across a panther. An experience, he said, that has only happened to him three times in his life. Ninety-nine percent of the time he has nothing to be afraid of. In fact, Fabiano is one of the most phlegmatic people I have ever met, rivaled only by other indigenous people and Buddhist monks.

"The Waorani don't stress," laughed Fausto, the guide who took me to visit the Waorani. "Every time I come to visit them I become so relaxed."

I couldn't help but agree. Here I was in the middle of the Amazon rainforest, brimming with mosquitoes and venomous snakes, a day's hike from the nearest town, a plane ride away from the nearest medical attention, and yet I couldn't remember the last time I felt so at ease.

The problem for people living in developed societies is that we have traded in the acute stressors of ancestral times for the chronic stress of modernity, and our bodies are not designed to deal with chronic stress. When we are chronically stressed, we don't heal as fast, we get sick more easily, women have irregular menstrual cycles, and men keep swearing, "This has never happened before" to their dissatisfied sexual partners.

But why are we perpetually stressed in an environment that is clearly safer than time past? Consider the case of captive animals. An orca, once free to roam the oceans in a pod of family and friends, but now kidnapped and forced to live in the equivalent of a bathtub, experiences this same perpetual stress response. While the lives of zoo animals are safer than in the wild -- they no longer have to worry about finding a steady stream of food, or fear getting eaten by a predator -- they tend to be far more distressed than their wild counterparts. This was especially true in the early days of zoos when animals were kept in cages resembling a prison cell in Alcatraz. Concrete walls and iron bars. Thankfully, over the past century, zookeepers have adopted a simple philosophy that has increased the well-being of their animals. They have come to realize that Mother Nature provides the blueprint for living well. An animal's habitat and lifestyle should resemble the natural environment in which its wild counterparts thrive. The zookeepers ensure that a gorilla's enclosure brims with green plant life, natural food sources and other gorillas. A polar bear is fed a natural diet of fresh fish, and its habitat is filled with cool water and dark caves.

It would be overdramatic to say that modern humans are zoo animals. But our stress response to red lights, office cubicles, screeching subway cars and social isolation is similar to that of a captive animal. There is such a massive mismatch between our natural environment and the modern world that our bodies have been put in a state of perpetual stress. We don't recognize this as abnormal since everyone we know suffers from it. A monkey raised in captivity has no idea that life need not be limited to tossing turds at well-dressed primates on the other side of the thick glass. Imagine its surprise when one day it is released into the wild and discovers that his new wild troupe has miles

86

upon miles of tree branches to swing and eat figs from. Modern humans who have gone to live with hunter-gatherer societies have noticed a similar freedom. After spending time living with the Hadza tribe in Tanzania, Michael Finkel wrote:

There are things I envy about the Hadza -- mostly, how free they appear to be. Free from possessions. Free of most social duties. Free from religious strictures. Free of many family responsibilities. Free from schedules, jobs, bosses, bills, traffic, taxes, laws, news, and money. Free from worry.

In evolutionary psychology, a "discord" is an adverse mismatch between the present way of life and the environment to which our genes are adapted. The human species burst on to the scene a few million years ago and lived in small bands of hunter-gatherer tribes up until the agricultural revolution around 10,000 years ago. Biologists believe that most of our uniquely human attributes evolved to solve reproductive problems during this period of HG existence and that our genes are best suited to this environment of evolutionary adaptedness (EEA). With the rise of agriculture, human beings went from living in small, close-knit bands of hunter-gatherer tribes to large agrarian societies, and our health and happiness may have been forever compromised.

The effect of small discords scattered throughout modern life can take their toll on the brain modules that regulate anxiety and depression. These modules are exercised by frequent use, meaning that the more stress, anxiety, and depression you experience, the more these negative states will become a salient part of your conscious life. Physically, activation of the hypothalamic-pituitary-adrenal axis, which causes stress, becomes more pronounced over time in people prone to experience stress. High activation of these negative modules leads to a situation where the natural positive mood of human beings may no longer be the default condition.

Then we use our great intelligence to make the problem worse. Unlike most animals, we get stressed out by simply imagining problems in the distant future. Through a strange quirk of our biology, imagined stress turns on the same physiological mechanisms that an acute stressor would in the reeds of the African bush. As we agonize over how to pay the rent, our heart rates go up, our blood pressure increases, and nervous energy flows through our body just the same as when confronted by a slithering black mamba. The more we activate the stress response, the more we worry. And the more we worry, the more we activate the stress response. And on and on it goes until we are no longer the confident, carefree creatures that is our birthright.

That rent bill isn't going away, and neither are the majority of problems we fret about in modern life. But if we turn down our baseline perpetual stress response, we can handle these problems with the Zen-like equanimity of our ancestors. To do this, we need to understand the discords between life in the EEA and life now. And most important -- what we can do about it.

Social Animals

In his book *Children of the Forest*, Kevin Duffy describes going out on a hunt with some Pygmies. Deep in the jungle they came across a red duiker antelope and sent their dogs after it. The antelope took flight and galloped away from the dogs, right into the trap where the diminutive Sukali was waiting, bow and arrow in hand. His shot hit the mark, but it wasn't a lethal wound, and when he pounced on the antelope, he was gored in the groin by the bucking antelope's sharp horns. Fortuitously, it was only a flesh wound, and although bleeding, he gamely continued in search of the next animal. Later, when the jolly hunters returned to camp after having bagged a large forest hog, the village celebrated with lots of singing and dancing. Sukali's gonad goring was re-enacted many times by two hunters, one playing Sukali and the other playing the antelope to the laughter of the entire tribe.

Homo sapiens are social animals. We have innate needs for friendship, intimacy, and a sense of community, just as we yearn for food and water. Studies of modern people show that interpersonal relationships are the single most important behavioral factor influencing well-being. At one end of the spectrum are those who are socially isolated. With them, a sense of loneliness releases stress hormones and causes blood pressure to rise. These lost souls are more likely to face all kinds of illnesses and a premature trip to the morgue. At the more fortunate end, what separates the very happiest among us from the mere happy isn't money, good looks, intelligence or social status. It is the quality of our relationships with friends, family, and romantic partners.

As many as 25 percent of Americans report they have no one close to confide in. People move away from their families and friends in search of employment. There they meet a romantic partner and begin a family of their own. The creation of a nuclear family far away from the support of grandparents and other relatives puts undue strain on these new parents. Relocating causes social bonds to become transient and weak, decreasing the length and intensity of friendships. This deprivation of intimate social support may be an explanation for the increasing rates of depression in modern man. This was not a problem our ancestors had to face.

Until a point roughly 10,000 years ago, humans lived in communities of no more than 150 to 200 people spread out over a large geographical area. These communities were further broken down into camps of about 25 to 50 people, consisting of five to ten families. Movement between camps was fluid. Maybe a teenage girl caught the fancy of a boy in the camp on the other side of the hill and went to go live with him. Or a person might go and stay with another camp for a while, before returning to his original camp. This community consisted of all the people you would know throughout your entire life. To meet a total stranger was a rare occurrence, a situation met with considerable trepidation.

How is it possible that hunter-gatherer communities dispersed all over the world ended up with a very similar number of members? Why wouldn't a group have 1,000 people? Or less, say a group of ten? One of the major reasons was the need for food. Hunting a large bear was not something you could do on your own; you needed a team of strong, able-bodied compatriots. But you couldn't have a group so large that there wasn't enough food to go around. That bear might have to provide a month's worth of protein for everyone in the group. Game was constantly on the move, and your band had to be ready to break camp as soon as the food in your area began to look sparse. Mobilizing a few dozen people for a task is a lot simpler than getting a thousand to agree on which direction to head off in. For these reasons, large-scale societies weren't feasible.

By necessity, HG groups were egalitarian. If one day you were the one who shot down the elk, social norms required you to share that meat with everyone else in the band. The basic principle was: "What goes around, comes around," because the next kill might be done by your cousin, and if he refused to share his meat in retaliation for you not sharing your kill, you would go hungry. With no money, few possessions and mandatory sharing of food, there were no social hierarchies to speak of. Everybody was on equal footing and attempts to place oneself above others were discouraged.

As Dan Everett puts it: "One of the strongest values of the Piraha is of no coercion. You simply do not tell others what to do."

In modern society, we are surrounded by people who have power over us -- bosses, teachers, those higher up the socioeconomic ladder. This is a constant source of stress. Studies have shown that people in low social-power positions display more negative affect and social inhibition than those with greater social power. Psychologists believe that the disconnect between our ancestral environment, where no one had dominance over anyone else, and modern life could theoretically lead to an abnormal expansion of the depression module in the brain. Personal autonomy, a trait highly praised in HG cultures, correlates strongly with levels of well-being.

Real Friends

Despite being fiercely autonomous, HG's maintained deep friendships that few of us will ever know. I'll illustrate this with a story of some HG's out on a dangerous hunt.

The thunderous plodding of a woolly mammoth burrowing through the bush was contrasted by the quiet whispers of the fur-clad Cro-Magnon. "Olog voha mug." "Vukh, Vukha, Simkala." That sort of thing. Swift With Foot leapt out of his crouching spot and rushed toward the elephant, spear in hand. The flint pierced the beast's jugular. Letting out a gigantic grunt, the animal bucked and knocked Swift With Foot to the ground. It moved in for the kill, preparing to stomp the young hunter into the dirt. Flying Bear and West Wind moved quickly. They thrust their spears into the elephant's hide. The mighty mammoth fell.

The three early humans let the scene engulf them in silence for a few moments before letting out rapturous screams and embracing each other. They were more than friends; they were cousins who lived together in the same band of hunter-gatherers. Every day they risked their lives for each other, and success depended on a loving bond fostered through many dangerous experiences.

People living in the relatively safe conditions of modern urban society often suffer from a dearth of strong friendships. Because the environment rarely exposes us to dangerous situations, we never experience the powerful bond that forms after a mutually felt adrenaline rush. It also deprives us of situations in which we may need our friends to be there to ensure our survival. Having a friend willing to step in and risk his safety to help you when things go south creates a fervent trust in one another. The people around you have saved your life. You have saved theirs. In HG society, survival depends on one another.

On this planet, we are all in this thing together. But in modern life this is hard to see. That annoying idiot who is taking way too long at the self-check-out counter may be a manager at a rubber company. His company supplies the material that your teenage daughter's car tires are made of. Those same tires that just yesterday came to an abrupt stop in the rain, saving your precious child from the oncoming tractor trailer. In that checkout line, however, we don't know this. Nor do we do think about the contributions that everyone else in that store makes on a daily basis to keep our society functioning. All we see is a fumbling buffoon who seems completely incapable of weighing his yams.

In a HG band, everyone's contribution is clear. My cousin there, he is the expert tracker. His wife knows just where to find the ripe strawberries. We know that all of the people we interact with throughout the day play a role in the functioning of the group and in our ability to survive. Hence, we are much more apt to forgive any slight personality quirk they might have in exchange for group harmony.

This makes me wonder about the genesis of our desire for fame and recognition. Back in ancestral times, everyone you would ever come across knew who you were. Also, in such a small society there was going to be something that you were the best at. You might be the Tiger Woods of stringing a bow and arrow, or the Serena Williams of basket-weaving. Everyone back then was a champion;

everyone was known by everyone. Is our desire to be the best in the world, to be famous, merely the result of that lack of recognition and skill that the modern world forces upon us?

Anthropologists are routinely awed by how much time tribal people spend talking to each other. Life in their villages is constant chatter, a running commentary on everything that is going on around them. The latest gossip. Thoughts about the weather and the animals. Reminiscing about great hunts. Predictions for the future. Minute details about what they ate, are eating, and will eat at future meals. All of this is punctuated by bouts of laughter.

Interpersonal communication is a skill that gets better with practice, just like anything else. Since the time they could first utter words, tribal people have been engaging in non-stop conversation day and night with other members of the tribe. Growing up, modern folk spend far less time in face to face conversation, and far more time all alone in our solitary work or lonely pursuits like video games. We are at a distinct disadvantage when it comes to being able to communicate with others.

That we may be rather dull conversationalists compared to tribal people became clear to me one night along the flowing waters of the Rio Napo, a tributary of the Amazon. I was staying with the Kichwa tribe, who set up their huts on stilts along the banks of the river. I, a Dutch couple, and a few members of the tribe were sitting around a campfire one night, imbibing a locally fermented drink and telling stories, when the oldest member of the tribe announced that it was time to sing. He broke out into a song in his native language, hitting a wide range of pitches, all with the melody of a professional *a cappella* singer. After belting out a few tunes, it was on to the next member of the tribe, who matched his feat. So did the tribesman after him. "Ok, who's next?" asked the old man, looking at me and the Dutch couple. We all declined. No way were we going on after the Amazonian Rat Pack.

What Can We Do?

It may seem that the disconnect between modern society and HG existence is just too great. Don't lose hope, my friend. Call up a buddy, get out of your house and go do something. I have personally conducted studies showing that active leisure activities correlate with positive well-being, while passive leisure activities like watching television and browsing the internet do not. If you are choosing between a night of sitting on the couch alone or going to a bonfire with some friends, don't let the minor inconveniences of having to get off your butt, shell out a few bucks, and travel a small distance get the best of you. It's almost always worth it in the end. Even introverts report feeling better when engaging in active social activities rather than being alone.

Get involved in communities that interest you. The Danish know this secret: Denmark is often reported to be the happiest country in the world. The majority of Danes belong to some association, like the cold-water swim club, handball team, or a volunteer group. Be like them. Find something you like and join a group of people doing that.

The benefits of having extended family around to help rear children cannot be understated. Kids are genetically programmed to be around more family members than just their parents; cousins provide great opportunities to make deep friendships, and grandparents can act as the wise elders of the tribal group that all our ancestors were privy to. They are also cost-effective babysitters.

The Awakened Ape

Your health and well-being are in large part a function of the quality of your social circle. Studies have shown that a person's happiness can be affected by up to three degrees of separation. That is, the friends of your friends of your friends. If you have a happy friend that lives within a mile of you, it increases the probability of your being happy by 25 percent. Happiness is contagious. So do your best to surround yourself with positive influences, primarily people you enjoy being around.

Pristine Health

European explorers were awed by the shockingly high level of health they found in aboriginal cultures around the world. Here is Captain Cook, writing about the native Maoris of New Zealand in 1772:

It cannot be thought strange that these people enjoy perfect and uninterrupted health. In all our visits to their towns, where young and old, men and women, crowd about us, prompted by the same curiosity that carried us to look at them, we never saw a single person who appeared to have any bodily complaint, nor among the numbers that we have seen naked did we perceive the slightest eruption upon the skin, or any marks that an eruption had left behind... A further proof that human nature is untainted with disease is the great number of old men that we saw...(who) appeared to be very ancient, yet none of them were decrepit; and though not equal to the young in muscular strength, were not a whit behind them in cheerfulness and vivacity.

While staying with the Waorani tribe, I asked an elderly woman what life was like pre-contact, before they were discovered by the modern world. She said it was wonderful, and no one ever got sick. She wasn't exaggerating. When the Waorani were first stumbled upon by first-world types in the 1950s, studies showed them to be totally free from hypertension, heart disease, cancer, anemia, the common cold, polio, pneumonia, smallpox, chicken pox, typhus, syphilis, tuberculosis, malaria or serum hepatitis.

These groups were by no means uncommon. In fact, they were the norm for what the early explorers and scientists found when they came across native tribes untroubled by the intrusion of modern man. These people rarely, if ever, suffered from cancer, diabetes, allergies, asthma, tooth caries, stroke, heart disease, depression or even acne. The cause of the vast majority of diseases we currently suffer from are not endemic to the human species, but arise from a lifestyle unsuitable to our genetic makeup.

The rapid changes that came with the invention of agriculture and animal husbandry roughly 10,000 years ago came too swiftly for the human body to adapt. Diet-related chronic diseases account for the majority of deaths in the United States, with heart disease, stroke and cancer causing over one million deaths per year. Up to 65 percent of the adult population in western societies is afflicted with a diet-related morbidity. Yet these illnesses are almost unheard of in hunter-gatherer populations eating off the land.

The rise of infectious diseases was another unexpected consequence of the development of agriculture. The incidence of malaria, perhaps the deadliest killer of all time, rose significantly after the agrarian revolution in Africa. Mosquitoes, the carriers of the parasitic protozoan that causes malaria, found more bodies to infect in the increasingly dense and populated cultures that sprang up when people abandoned their nomadic ways to settle down and grow their food. To compound the problem, early agrarian cultures built or lived near numerous small water sources, the breeding grounds of mosquitoes.

Small, foraging societies were spared from most of the infectious diseases that have afflicted mankind throughout modern history. These diseases came initially from animals that were bred in captivity and then passed on their germs to their handlers. Viruses need hosts to survive. The flu lives on because somewhere in the world there is someone who has some version of the flu. If all living creatures were free of the flu, the flu virus would become extinct. If a viral bug infects an isolated tribe of 100 people, those infected will either die or recover. If everyone dies, the virus will no longer have any hosts to infect, and it will die along with its victims.

Because these tribes often lived in isolated communities, they never came into contact with anyone who had the flu or even the common cold. The Waorani provide a perfect example of a tribe that was once isolated and free from most infectious diseases until they came into contact with the outside world. Such tribes remain free from these annoying and sometimes deadly viral infections until a person from an agriculturally-based society turns up. Carrying the deadly bug, he can unwittingly commit genocide on an entire race of people with a simple cough, infecting natives who have no natural immunity to these microscopic foreign invaders.

Skeptic: Wait a minute, buddy, if I know anything about cavemen, it's that they all died by the age of thirty!

A: This is by far the most common myth about our ancestors. No, they didn't all die by the age of thirty. This misconception comes about because of the different way we interpret statistics. While it is true that the mean age of death in these societies may have been as low as the thirties and forties, that does not mean that most people died when they were thirty or forty.

To give an example, my father is one of nine children. Of the nine, six are still alive, and three have passed away. Two of those died in infancy, one during childbirth, the other at the age of one. The third to die, the oldest sibling, succumbed to brain cancer at age fifty-seven. If we assume that the surviving siblings live to the average age of death for people in their relative cultures (U.S. males living to age seventy-eight) and Spanish women (where my aunts live: eighty-five years), then we get a mean age of death for the family of sixty. Yet only one of the nine siblings would have died at an age anywhere near sixty, while the other six siblings will have lived to an average age of eighty. It is the two infant deaths that significantly bring down the average.

Infant mortality in hunter-gatherer tribes was thirty times higher than in modern society and childhood mortality one hundred times higher. One of the main culprits for this high rate of infant mortality was the common practice of infanticide. It is believed that somewhere between fifteen and fifty percent of all young babies died from infanticide.

Skeptic: Infanticide? What the hell?

A: In a world without modern medicine, only the strongest were able to survive. Ask yourself: Would you have made it out of childhood if you had never seen a doctor? I know that I had a terrible case of pneumonia at age one, and who's to say that without the help of modern medicine I would have survived. If a baby is born unhealthy, or if the tribe is going through a time of limited resources, or if the mother already has too many other babies to nurse and care for, the likelihood of this new, weak and sick child surviving to adulthood would be poor. Killing the newborn now would save her from the greater grief of seeing this child die in a few years time. Infanticide was simply considered a very late abortion, in a time when what we consider abortion wasn't possible.

But let's say that you are a hunter-gatherer that has survived your childhood and made it to age fifteen. To what age would you be most likely to live? A study entitled "Longevity Among Hunter-Gatherers: A Cross-Cultural Examination" found that the modal age of death for adults in extant hunter-gatherer tribes was seventy-two. What this means is that if you made it to the age of fifteen, you were fairly likely to live into your seventies. This, only a few years shorter than the average lifespan of people in well-off modern society, and without the help of modern medicine.

Skeptic: So what *did* kill the hunter-gatherers?

A: Anthropologists have studied a group of hunter-gatherers called the Hiwi, who live in the savannah plains of Venezuela and Columbia. Due to the prevalence of malaria, and war with Venezuelans encroaching on their territory, they have one of the shortest life expectancies of extant hunter-gatherer/hunter-horticulturist tribes. But we can see from the data that what they died from was not the same maladies we in modern society suffer from. We can look at the chart chronicling the actual deaths of members of the Hiwi tribe and see exactly what killed them. Most interesting is the data collected from pre-contact times (that is pre-contact with modern society, as the tribe had contact with primitive farming groups for hundreds of years). This, it would seem, would be the most telling data regarding a natural hunter-gatherer tribe.

169 deaths were recorded:

Infectious disease (Malaria, respiratory infection, diarrhea, measles) = 70
War (with each other or Venezuelans) = 33
Infanticide = 13
Congenital infant death (birth trauma and other childbirth deaths) = 12
Environmental Hazard = 7
Human Caused Accident = 7
Suicide = 3
Organic and pathological conditions (heart problems, cancer, liver problems, "swallowed tongue") = 1
Nutritional deficiencies (starvation or malnourished) = 0

As you can see, the Hiwi did not die deaths that are ubiquitous in modern society. Cancer, heart disease, diabetes and other afflictions of that sort were completely unheard of amongst the Hiwi. Most of the members of the tribe died from infectious diseases, spawned by the agrarian revolution, having made their way into nearly every nook and cranny across the globe. These traditional societies know nothing about microbes, hand washing and other sanitary practices, and often attributed death from infectious diseases to evil spirits or witchcraft. Violent death amongst the Hiwi is abnormally high. The reasons for this are not endemic to their nature but due to the circumstances modernity has forced upon them. They now dwell in a reservation near another Hiwi tribe with which there has long been historical tension. The land area is small, which leads to conflicts over resources, particularly from Venezuelan ranchers who try to steal their land. In South America, it is a common problem for aboriginal people to experience violence at the hands of ranchers, loggers and other settled people who would like use of the land and ignore government restrictions.

Among the African tribes of the !Kung and the Hadza, violence is not a major cause of death, with only five Hadza reported being murdered over a 15-year period. Three of those murders came at the hands of nearby ranchers, in retaliation for the Hadza having killed a few of their cows. Among the Hadza, there were two deaths due to animal attacks, one by a hyena and the other from a snake bite. Overall, the main causes of death among contemporary hunter-gatherers, hunter-horticulturists, and related small-scale societies are respiratory illnesses such as pneumonia, tuberculosis and bronchitis, followed by gastrointestinal illnesses. Could these gastrointestinal ailments also have been exacerbated by the encroachment of modern civilization? Considering that African tribes often have to deal with the sanitary runoff from nearby farming villages in their water supplies and that the Amazonian tribes are forced to live deep in the jungle, where tropical parasites are rampant, it seems like a good bet.

It is highly possible that our prehistoric ancestors enjoyed longer average lifespans than modern-day hunter-gatherers. Not only would they have been largely free from infectious diseases and have suffered less violence and fewer gastrointestinal problems. They also would have owned prime real estate. The reason hunter-gatherers still exist at all is because they have been pushed to the very ends of the earth, where nobody wants to live: the Amazon, the Arctic and the African desert. Tens of thousands of years ago, people would not settle down in an area so prevalent with mosquitos, nor would people have to war with neighboring farmers over land space as the Hiwi often do. Our ancestors would have been free to roam the most fertile lands, far removed from the diseases of civilization, and free to enjoy the most pristine health ever known to man.

A Natural Diet

The very fabric of your skin, hair, and internal organs is woven from the nutrients you ingest. Is it any wonder that diet will play such an important role in your well-being? I've already described the pristine health of traditional societies. These same people, upon contact with the white man, and after adopting his culinary habits, will quickly and dramatically fall ill.

Nowhere is this more obvious than in the Pacific islands. Once so admired for their beautiful bodies and health that the first explorers thought they had stumbled upon Eden, their descendants are now the most obese people on the face of the earth. Having traded in their traditional diet of yam, coconuts, fruits and fish for deadly modern processed foods, the health of these islanders has plummeted. In some places, up to 90 percent of the population is overweight, and half the population, perhaps more, is obese. In a truly terrifying statistic, 40 percent of the Pacific island population has been diagnosed with a non-communicable disease such as diabetes, heart disease or hypertension. These diseases account for 75 percent of the deaths in the region. And while the inhabits of the Pacific islands provide the most drastic example of the modern health epidemic, they certainly aren't the only ones suffering.

Obesity-related illnesses kill over 8,000 people every single day. The lack of public outcry over this is bewildering. Maybe it's because everyone's mouths are too filled with fudge brownies to say anything. The health consequences of obesity are disastrous. They include, but are not limited to, heart disease, cancer, asthma, stroke, dementia, Type II diabetes, and birth defects. Worldwide, obesity is the leading cause of death. And it is totally preventable.

The saddest of all is childhood obesity, which has doubled over the last 30 years, and quadrupled amongst adolescents. By 2012, one-third of all children were overweight or obese. The consequences to the health of our children have been devastating. Kids are now suffering from all sorts of cancers, hypertension and other heart problems that previous generations didn't think were possible. Type II diabetes used to be called Adult-Onset Diabetes because it was something that only occurred once you were fully grown. Now children get it. An obese child is far more likely to become an obese adult than a thin child. Even if an obese child grows up and makes every effort to lose weight, the effects of being obese as a child will still linger, as the body never fully recovers. Allowing your kids to become fat and thereby permanently damaging their health is child abuse, plain and simple.

The toll of obesity doesn't simply affect the overweight. The latest estimates are that obesity could cost up to $344 billion per year in the United States alone by 2018. That's a lot of money that thin people are being forced to cough up in the form of taxes and increased insurance premiums. A concerted effort is needed by all of us to tackle this problem, and it begins with education.

There is a popular misconception that obesity is determined by genetics, and hence, a fatalist acceptance of an oval-shaped physique. While genetics plays a role in everything, with the rare exception of certain diseases, it is no one's destiny to be obese. In the year 1900 only one in 150 people was obese. Now 35% of Americans over the age of 20 are obese, and the number is skyrocketing. The problem is environmental not genetic. The human genome has not undergone such dramatic change in only a few generations that we now look like a completely different animal.

When scientists looked at the body composition of the hunter-gatherer Hadza tribe of Tanzania they did not find a single member of the tribe to be overweight! The fattest person in the entire community was a woman with a BMI of 23.9, while the CDC's criteria for overweight is 25. The mean age of women in the tribe was 40, and yet the average BMI for a Hadza woman was a slim 20.2, with a body fat percentage of 20.9 percent. By comparison, the average body fat percentage for women in western society is 37 percent. The Hadza men came in at a lean 20.3 BMI and 13 percent body fat. The Hadza are not outliers, getting fat is just not something HG's do or did beyond the rare occasion of bulking up before a foreseen famine. Human beings are not meant to be fat, not as children, not as adults and not in our golden years.

What exactly is the problem? Why is modern processed food so bad for us, while traditional diets are healthy? For the same reason a cow can survive on grass and we can't. There are foods that we are meant to eat, and there are foods we are not.

The philosophy of the Paleo diet is that humans are genetically adapted to the diet of our Paleolithic ancestors. For two million years, human beings roamed the planet in search of wild fruits and vegetables while hunting game meats. It was only with the advent of agriculture that cereal grains, dairy, refined sugars, refined cooking oils and alcohol became staples of the modern diet. In fact, 70 percent of the total energy consumed by citizens of the United States comes from these new energy sources. This massive divergence from our ancestral diet to the modern diet of processed foods is the reason for the skyrocketing rates of obesity, diabetes, heart disease and some forms of cancer. Sounds like a solid theory, but is it backed up by science? Yes, it is.

Observational Evidence

Luckily for us, there are people alive today that remain uninfluenced by the trappings of the modern food industry. They are hard to find, but they are out there. One population of such people lives on the Island of Kitava off the coast of Papua New Guinea.

The Kitavans eat a diet of root vegetables, fruits, coconuts, leafy vegetables and fish. Dr. Staffan Lindeberg and his colleagues studied the Kitavans to ascertain their levels of health. They were found to have no incidences of heart disease, stroke, diabetes or even acne. The elderly showed no signs of dementia or memory loss.

A meta-analysis of the health profile of modern day hunter-gather civilizations, including the Bushmen of Africa, the Yonomamo and Xingu tribes of the Amazon, and the Kitavans found these tribal societies to have:

1. Lower blood pressure
2. No association between blood pressure and age
3. Persistent excellent insulin sensitivity

4. Lower body mass, no incidences of people being overweight or obese

5. Lower waist-to-height ratios

6. Greater maximum oxygen consumption

7. Better vision

8. Better bone health

Among others

Diet and Mental Health

In recent years, numerous studies have demonstrated the effect of diet on mental health. In 2011, a study of over 5,000 Norwegians revealed that those who ate a traditional diet of meat and vegetables had lower levels of anxiety, depression, and bipolar disorder compared to those who ate either a modern Western diet of processed and fast foods, or a group of people eating a so-called "healthy" vegetarian diet of salads and tofu.

The relationship between diet and brain chemistry is incredibly complex. What follows is a simplified explanation of what goes on in your brain, and an analysis of the chemicals responsible for certain moods. The human brain contains about 100 billion neurons or nerve cells. These cells communicate with each other through chemical and electrical signals. The process by which they do this is by sending neurotransmitters from one neuron to another across the synapse (a small gap between neurons). These neurotransmitters are chemical messengers that carry information from one neuron to the next. Many types of neurotransmitters exist, but for your well-being the most essential are dopamine and serotonin.

Dopamine is the brain's reward system. Your body will release a surge of dopamine when you anticipate a rewarding behavior such as sex and eating. In lab studies, mice that were depleted of dopamine could not be motivated to find food that was close by and would starve to death without the intervention of the experimenters. Dopamine drives behavior to accomplish goals. If you are low on dopamine, you might feel lethargic, have trouble concentrating and generally feel unmotivated. People with ADHD are treated with drugs that activate dopamine systems in the brain. Drugs like cocaine and meth have similar effects on the dopamine system. In these drugs, over-activation of the dopamine system can lead to long-term depletion of dopamine receptors. Sugary, processed foods work much the same way. A 2001 study published in *The Lancet* showed that obese people have fewer dopamine receptors than people of normal weight, and that the fattest people had even fewer dopamine receptors than their less obese, but still corpulent cohorts.

When it comes to well-being, Serotonin is the most famous chemical. The most commonly prescribed drugs for depression, such as Prozac and Paxil, are Selective Serotonin Re-uptake Inhibitors (SSRI's). These drugs are thought to work by blocking the reabsorption of serotonin in the sending nerve cell. When one nerve cell sends information to the next and that cell is using serotonin as its chemical messenger, the serotonin crosses over the synapse from the sending neuron to the receiving neuron, delivers its message and then can return to the sending neuron. Back in the sending neuron the serotonin is in position to act as a messenger again for the next nerve signal.

Those with depression may have low levels of serotonin, and the serotonin that they do have may be reabsorbed too soon. As a result, the communication between the brain cells is impaired. What an SSRI does is block the reabsorption of serotonin, leaving more serotonin in the synapse. When the amount of serotonin in the synapse is sufficient, communication between nerve cells will improve, and depression may be alleviated. Serotonin is also thought to improve sleep, as well as reduce anxiety and irritability.

If your serotonin levels are low, you can take an SSRI, which is basically a band aid, and only works for some people, or you can figure out why your serotonin levels are low in the first place and fix the problem by solving the root cause. Many factors influence low serotonin levels, but here we are interested only in diet-related causes. One of the major building blocks of serotonin is the amino acid tryptophan. If you don't get enough tryptophan in your diet, there is reduced synthesis of serotonin in the brain. But it is not as simple as just adding tryptophan, tryptophan needs vitamin B6 to make serotonin, so you need more of that vitamin as well. Because these chemicals work in concert, it is better to get them from whole foods than taking supplements.

Sea lion kidney holds the record for the food with the highest content of tryptophan. If you know of a good supplier of that, pass it on to me. Otherwise, you can eat more conventional foods such as spinach, crab, lobster, fish, pork, goat and eggs. Vitamin B6 is one of the most common deficiencies for people who eat the Western diet. However, it is easily obtained by eating tuna, turkey, beef, chicken, salmon, sweet potatoes, spinach, and bananas.

Inadequate levels of magnesium are also thought to reduce the amount of serotonin in the brain. One study showed that in diabetic patients, treating them with magnesium was just as effective as antidepressants in treating depression. Green leafy vegetables such as spinach and Swiss chard as well as pumpkin and sesame seeds are your best bet for getting magnesium through your diet.

Gut Bacteria

In 2009, a remote tribe of Yanomami Indians were going about their daily lives of hunting and gathering in the mountainous region of the Amazon, just as they had been for thousands of years, when a team of microbiologists from the NYU School of Medicine and the Venezuelan government suddenly appeared. The Indians knew that the outside world existed, and had invented words to describe the airplanes they saw fly overhead, but they had never been contacted by modern people before. Now here they were, these other humans with their magical flying machines right there in the Yanomami village! What could they possibly want? Poop, apparently. The microbiologists said hello, asked if they could have a few samples of Yanomami droppings, climbed back into their helicopters and vanished.

Hippocrates said that all disease begins in the gut. Now, over 2,000 years later, we are just beginning to understand the importance of the microbiome -- the 100 trillion bacteria that make their home in the human body. A western diet full of processed foods and sugar negatively alters the balance between good and bad bacteria.

Hunter-gatherers don't have this problem. Their digestive tracts are flourishing with all sorts of microbes helpful in immune function, digesting carbohydrates, and acting as prebiotics to name just a few of the benefits. The Yanomami were found to have 50 percent more ecological diversity than the average American.

The modern diet is one cause of our famished microbiome, but our cleanliness is another. There is a trade-off here. HG's live outside nearly 24/7, have few scruples about eating certain animal parts raw, drink from streams and don't use soap. Many scientists feel that our sterility is the cause of overactive immune responses such as allergies. With nothing else to do, our immune response goes on red alert in the presence of benign invaders like tree pollen. Studies of infants found that those with less diverse gut bacteria were more likely to have food allergies to milk, peanuts, and eggs. Lower levels of certain types of gut bacteria have even been linked to autism. On the other hand, our purified drinking water and hand-washing habits ensure that we don't die from intestinal parasites.

How can we safely improve our gut bacteria? We can eat lots of fruits, vegetables and fermented foods like sauerkraut. The more adventurous can get a fecal matter transplant. Think I'm joking? Anthropologists working with the Hadza tribe have been taking samples of the tribesman's dung and then inserting the feces into their own rectums using a turkey baster. Now with that attractive image clearly in your mind, let me tell you what you should be eating.

Good To Eat
- Fish (preferably wild caught)
- Other seafood
- Beef (preferably grass-fed beef)
- Poultry
- Pig
- Other game meats
- Vegetables
- Root vegetables
- Fruits
- Nuts
- Seeds

• Eggs

Foods to Avoid
• Processed foods
• Grains
• Refined sugar
• Processed oils

Grey-Area Foods (depends on individual variation. Eliminate these foods from your diet at first and then slowly let them back in and see how they affect you.)
• Dairy (if you are not lactose-intolerant). Should be whole fat, and better if fermented, such as cheeses and yogurts.
• Rice
• Potatoes (Modern potatoes differ significantly from their wild tuber counterparts. Most Paleo diet gurus recommend sweet potatoes instead. Personally I'll eat any type of baked potato. Yum.)

Fun Fitness

The hunt will begin at 8 a.m, once everyone has woken up, had a smoke and sharpened their arrows. When you live under the remorseless Tanzanian sun, it is best to catch your breakfast before the afternoon heat sets in. Around the campfire, the men chat about where they are going, what they will hunt, and hopefully, kill. Some will go together in search of wild honey. They will build a fire to distract the bees with smoke, and then stick their bare hands inside the tree and pull out the delicious treat. Others will hunt alone. The Hadza have no leaders, and even boys are allowed to go off with bows and arrows in hand wherever their whim takes them.

How far they will travel depends on how fast they find prey. The average Hadza walks five miles a day, but on days where food is hard to find, it is not unheard of to tread through the bush for 15 to 20 miles. There are no electric outlets in the red clay near their camp to plug in a refrigerator. If you want to eat, you have to go out and get it.

Here's a dirty little secret about exercise. *It's unnatural.* Our hunter-gatherer ancestors didn't do it. What do I mean? Haven't I've already explained that our ancestors looked smashingly fit? The issue is one of semantics, the dictionary definition of exercise being "activity requiring physical effort, carried out especially to sustain or improve health and fitness." Our ancestors were very active and burned lots of calories, but they did all this hunting, gathering, logging buckets of water and chopping wood, not to improve their physical fitness, but in the service of another goal: survival. A HG didn't go for a jog to improve his triathlon time. He and his companions jogged for hours, hunting large game. Women didn't do squats to make their butts look nice; they did squats while picking up a basket of sweet potatoes.

It would be crazy for a HG to waste precious energy exercising when food sources were limited, and muscle soreness might hinder his ability to walk 20 km the next day while carrying a carcass on his shoulders. Despite never going to the gym, the average daily physical activity level of the HG was far greater and much more varied than that of your typical Westerner.

The daily movement of a HG might go as follows. Men would pick up their bows and arrows, walk miles through the tough terrain of the jungle or bush, ducking under branches, hopping over streams, until they found the animal they were hunting. Upon encountering the beast, there could be an intense chase, requiring all-out sprinting. Once the creature was subdued, the HG would carry it back to camp. There the animal would be skinned and chopped up. Women would also go on long walks to areas where vegetables grew. They would dig up the plants and carry the heavy baskets back, often with a young child strapped to their torsos!

Besides acquiring food, HG's had to engage in the maintenance activities of life, weaving baskets, sharpening blades, chopping and carrying firewood, making clothing and building huts. At night, they might dance for hours.

They were the original cross-trainers, and it showed in their slim, fit bodies.

This physical exertion is not only necessary for sexy midsections but for mental health as well. A study conducted by Duke University took clinically depressed patients and put them into two different treatment groups. One group took the anti-depressant medication Zoloft, and the other group simply engaged in brisk walking three times a week for thirty minutes. After four months both the Zoloft group and the walking group had significantly improved their depression compared to those taking a placebo. However, in a six-month follow-up, those who had taken Zoloft were three times more likely to have their depression return than those who were exercising. Merely walking is a better treatment for depression than the best chemical products our genius scientists can come up with. More vigorous exercise is even better.

A review study on the effects of exercise on mental health found that exercising is a robust treatment for psychological conditions ranging from anxiety disorders to schizophrenia. Conversely, the lack of exercise is associated with the development of these very same disorders. Even if you aren't suffering from a classically defined mental illness, exercising is imperative to boosting mood, enhancing attention span and improving cognitive ability. Science has disproven the dumb jock stereotype. It's the kids who exercise that have the highest mental functioning, and adults who maintain physical fitness are far more likely to age gracefully, both in terms of appearance and mental ability.

A female friend once spoke to me about her dilemma; she needed to get in shape, but she hated to exercise. This is a common complaint amongst today's more sedentary types. They whine that exercising is painful, a chore, something they don't find enjoyable. I asked my friend what she did for exercise.

"Oh, I get on the treadmill and jog for 45 minutes. It's so boring. I hate it!"

"You're right," I told her. "That's a terrible way to exercise." Running on a treadmill is monotonous, it doesn't engage the total body, and it is a joyless, solitary endeavor. All of which would have been completely foreign to how her female ancestors moved.

While men in HG tribes might hunt alone, the women gathered together in groups for safety reasons. A female human being is a large, powerful ape in her own right, and a group of them is enough to deter predatory animals from viewing them as an easy lunch. Using our ancestors as a guide, women should work out with other females, and the exercises should be varied and involve not only aerobic conditioning but also weightlifting. Group classes at the gym can be great for this, but keep it diverse. Don't just do spin, don't just do yoga, do both, and add some weights as well. Dancing, from Zumba to tango, mimics the hours our grandest of grandmothers spent twirling and jiving around the campfire.

Humans also have an innate need to compete, especially men. Our ancestors exerted physical effort with the goal of defeating an opponent. Sometimes alone, but generally as part of a team. Sometimes this opponent was an animal, sometimes an enemy in war. Men like to win battles. Thus sports, both team, and individual, are the most psychologically rewarding forms of exercise for fellas. If we can do this outside, under the shining sun, even better.

It's also essential for us to keep our activities varied. By doing so we will master the four cornerstones of fitness and athleticism: having great cardio, being strong, being flexible, and being skilled. Go for a long hike with a group of friends. Or grab two 50-pound sandbags, hand one to a buddy and see who can walk a mile the fastest. Take a hot yoga class. Play basketball. Learning a martial art can satisfy that innate desire to be a warrior and protector.

No matter who you are, if exercise isn't fun, you are either doing it wrong or your attitude needs work. When we are lifting weights, our muscles require extra oxygen and nutrients. To accomplish this, the body sends a rush of blood to the muscle. Bodybuilders call this "the pump." Arnold Schwarzenegger described the feeling as follows:

The greatest feeling you can get in a gym, or the most satisfying feeling you can get in the gym is...The Pump. Let's say you train your biceps. Blood is rushing into your muscles and that's what we call The Pump. Your muscles get a really tight feeling, like your skin is going to explode any minute, and it's really tight -- it's like somebody blowing air into it, into your muscle. It just blows up, and it feels really different. It feels fantastic. It's as satisfying to me as, uh, coming is, you know? As, ah, having sex with a woman and coming. And so can you believe how much I am in heaven? I am like, uh, getting the feeling of coming in a gym, I'm getting the feeling of coming at home, I'm getting the feeling of coming backstage when I pump up, when I pose in front of 5,000 people, I get the same feeling, so I am coming day and night. I mean, it's terrific. Right? So you know, I am in heaven.

Get Up, Stand Up; Stand Up for Your Life.

Even if you exercise, sitting will still kill you. All that vigorous training you do isn't enough to offset the 9.3 hours we spend each day on our rumps. Modern life is one long, rarely-interrupted sitting session from the moment we wake up to the moment we turn in for the night. We eat breakfast while sitting down in our kitchen, then we sit in our cars until we get to work, where we spend the next eight hours mostly sitting in front of a computer, and when it's time to leave, we get back in our cars, and back to the dinner table, before finally plopping down on the couch for some primetime television. Studies indicate that prolonged sitting will take as many years off your life as smoking. One provocative finding published in the *British Journal of Sports Medicine* found that after age 25, every hour you sit in front of the television takes 22 minutes off your life expectancy.

Deep down inside, we know that all this lethargy isn't good for us. Mom has been yelling at us not to be a couch potato since we were tots. But what exactly goes wrong in the body while we are sitting? Let's start with the heart. During a prolonged sit, blood flows sluggishly and can clog the heart with the fatty acids that your muscles aren't burning. Those of us who sit the most have higher blood pressure, higher cholesterol levels, and a far higher chance of dying from a heart attack.

Another problem caused by sitting is an enormous increase in our risk of getting diabetes. When we sit, our plasma insulin and glucose levels rise, since our idle muscle cells don't respond as effectively to insulin. Some scientists theorize that this excess insulin in our system is also the reason that sitting has been linked to colon, breast, and other cancers.

Furthermore, sitting can lead to muscle degeneration. Slumped in a chair, our core and leg muscles aren't getting used, which can cause a host of other muscular problems downstream as we try to compensate for these flabby muscles. We also become inflexible in our necks, our spines, and especially our all-important hip flexors.

Most important as regards to our mental health, prolonged sitting leads to brain fog. When we are up and moving blood flows through the body and into the brain, causing a release of alertness and feel good chemicals. Nietzsche, ahead of his time as always, once quipped: "All great thoughts are conceived by walking."

To combat the effects of sitting, you need to get up and move around every 30 minutes. Take a little walk around the building, go up and down a few stairs, throw a few kicks and punches when no one's looking. In one study, people who simply walked for two minutes after every hour of sitting lowered their risk of premature death by 33 percent.

Posture

There are indigenous cultures that report essentially no back pain, the result of the natural ways in which they hold their bodies. When studying the spinal cords of these indigenous people, we notice something different than what our modern anatomy books tell us about the shape of the spine. Their spines are J-shaped instead of the modern American S-shape. The S-shape refers to modern man's tendency to slump forward, with the shoulders drooped and the neck sticking out in front of the back. This isn't natural. Instead, it's a result of the poor posture humans have recently adopted. Our ancestors didn't sit in chairs with backrests. When they sat, they did so on rocks, logs, and tree stumps, or just on the ground with their legs crossed. Often they simply did a full squat and rested in that pose. Indigenous cultures and even Leonardo Da Vinci drawings show a spine that is straight all the way down to the base before it curves to make the buttocks stick out.

Remarkably, sitting up straight influences what we remember. In one experiment at San Francisco State University, students who were told to sit with good posture found it easier to recall positive memories from time past. Poor posture has the opposite effect: When experimenters had participants walk around slouched over, they found that their mood darkened and their energy levels waned. Another group, told to skip, saw their energy levels increase. You might want to be discreet about using this tip at the office.

"Uh, Bob, what's that you you're doing in there? Is that skipping?"

"Sure is, Phil. Keeps my energy levels up!"

Constantly reminding yourself to stand up straight may help, but what you really need to do is stretches and exercises that will align the muscles and take care of any imbalances. The fastest and easiest exercise to correct for your slumped-over shoulders is to simply hang from a pull-up bar. Try to hang for 30 seconds at first, and then work your way up to longer times. Do this in the morning and you'll be walking around tall and proud all day long.

Next, you need to straighten your pelvis. Because of prolonged sitting, we tend to stand with the front of our pelvis leaning downwards, and the back of our pelvis raised. This causes a cascade of problems up and down the spine.

To correct for this, lie down on your back and put your feet up on a chair so that your thighs and torso are at a 90-degree angle, as well as another 90-degree angle between your shins and thighs. Place your hands about eight inches away from your body, with your palms facing the ceiling. Tuck in your chin a bit so that your neck isn't arched. This position will align our pelvic muscles, which the heels on our shoes cause to lean downwards, creating a chain reaction of spinal curvature all the way up through our necks. Just lay there for five minutes or so. I personally like to do breathing exercises or meditation while I'm in this position, killing two birds with one stone. You can also make use of the time by listening to relaxing music or a book on tape. Try it. You'll like it.

<u>Day and Night</u>

As I open my eyes to the rising summer sun, I have a ritual I do the first thing in the morning. Before making breakfast, before checking my phone and my email and getting on with the chores of the day, I get out of bed and pick up my yoga mat. I walk outside to my back deck, lay the mat on the ground and begin a series of yoga postures called "sun salutations." Stretching my limbs as the sun's rays beat upon my bare back, I feel energized. I am soaking up the awesome power from our nearest star. My muscles begin to loosen, my body calms down, and my mind feels alert and calm. The tone for the rest of the day has been set.

Today, we spend far too much time indoors: For the average American, at least 87 percent of the day. Considering that our ancestors spent nearly all their time outdoors, this marks quite a rupture with ancient life. This disconnect is absolutely terrible for our health and happiness.

A half-billion years ago, our microscopic ancestors began to develop a circadian rhythm -- the tone of their life -- setting and rising with the spin of the earth's axis to the glow of the sun's rays. We evolved chemical processes regulating our ability to function well in accordance with these astronomical facts. Exposure to the sun tells the brain to produce serotonin, helping us to be more focused and happy. Get your daily dose first thing in the morning and you are going to have a nice start to the day. Later, as the sun dips down below the horizon, our bodies anticipate the oncoming slumber, gradually lowering the core body temperature, releasing melatonin and the neurotransmitter adenosine, and easing us into a beautiful sleep. Modern life fails to honor the precious relationship with that astonishing yellow star, disrupting the natural balance in our lives by replacing sunlight with artificial bulbs, the great outdoors with the four-walled room, and the relaxing glow of the campfire before bedtime with hyper-stimulating TV, PC, cell phone and iPad screens. Our biological processes get thrown into disorder, leading to a society of fat, sickly, walking zombies, desperately clutching their cappuccinos like Golem's ring.

Vitamin D

My body is well adapted to the warm and sunny Mediterranean environment where my forefathers spent their days outside hunting and gathering and eventually farming. Despite my attempts to get as much sunlight as possible, the cold winters and cultural mores of the society which I now inhabit force me to cover my skin in clothing and spend far too much time indoors. My Vitamin D levels plummet to unsafe levels, and I must resort to taking supplements, which are helpful but cannot completely compensate for the lack of those missing, shining rays. When the sun does appear in all its glory during those frosty months it beckons me like the Sirens of yore, "Come, Jevan, never mind the chill air; take off your shirt, lay out and let my brilliant golden beams warm your body." And I acquiesce.

Recent studies show that worldwide over 1 billion people are vitamin D- deficient, and if you live in a northern climate (above Philadelphia), the odds are better than 50/50 that you are one of these folks. If you have dark skin, you are particularly susceptible. This is no small matter. Vitamin D deficiency increases the risk of bone diseases like osteoporosis, as well as heart disease, stroke, multiple sclerosis, depression and impacts the strength of your immune system, making it more likely that you will catch an infection. A study of Japanese children found that those who took a 1,200 IU pill of vitamin D daily were 40 percent less likely to catch the flu that year than a placebo group. In the elderly, those with low vitamin D levels are far more likely to suffer from impaired understanding, dementia and Alzheimer's.

Skeptic: But wait a minute; if I spend all that time in the sun, am I not susceptible to skin cancer?

A. Skin cancer is indeed a risk for those who spend too much time in the sun, particularly those of lighter complexion. Their genes evolved to accommodate the gloomy, overcast lands of northern Europe, not the scolding beaches of Florida, which turns their skin into a leathery crisp. How to know if you are getting too much sun? Well, your skin evolved a great mechanism for such detection. It burns. Get as much sun as you can, but stop before you turn into a lobster. The cancer risk of not getting enough sunlight might outweigh that of getting too much. Vitamin D has a protective effect against colon, breast, prostate, and ovarian cancers.

Sleep

As the sun fell and darkness descended on the ancestral world, the lack of artificial light cued the body that sleep was not far away. These long periods of darkness, 12 hours a day on average, meant there was plenty of time for slumber parties.

And that is exactly what our ancestors did. Families slept together in a single hut, the whole tribe might pass out together in one large dwelling or by the fire. Anthropological reports of modern tribes show that some people do not fall asleep for eight hours straight, but awaken at different points in the night, make love, laugh, stoke the fire, and then go back to sleep. At any point in the night, there is usually someone in the tribe who is awake. These habits are a carryover from our simian days, when dangerous predators lurked in the darkness. Some recent sleep studies of hunter-gatherers challenge this view, and report that the tribes slept steadily throughout the night and did not awaken for substantial periods of time, instead dozing the whole night through. Whatever the case, our ancestors slept well. Two of the tribes whose sleep habits have been most thoroughly examined by scientists, the Tsimane of Bolivia and the San of Namibia, have no word in their language that corresponds to insomnia. Only two percent of the members of these tribes report having trouble sleeping more than one night a year.

There might not be anything more important to your mental well-being than getting consistent, high-quality sleep. After a bad night's sleep, our whole operating system runs inefficiently. We can't pay attention, we don't encode what we learned that day into long-term memory, we are quicker to feel irritated and angry, more prone to mood swings, more likely to make poor decisions. Prolonged sleep deprivation has been linked to anxiety, depression and even suicide.

Sleep is just as important for physical health. During the night, our body repairs any injured tissues, regulates hormones, adjusts insulin levels and keeps our heart and blood vessels functioning properly. Obesity, heart attacks, stroke and diabetes are all linked to sleep deprivation. Our immune system is similarly impaired, making us more likely to catch a cold from the slob coughing into his hands and then touching a public doorknob. When we are tired, any lingering infections we have just won't seem to go away.

We don't have to miss major amounts of sleep for any of this to occur either. Just an hour or two of missed sleep for a few days in a row and these deleterious effects will show up. You have to make sleep a top priority in your life. You should wake up feeling refreshed and energetic after a night of quality sleep. If you feel like you are dragging yourself through the mud until you have your coffee, you aren't getting quality sleep.

Here are a few tips for improved sleep.

Avoid Stimulation

Limit your intake of caffeine to the morning. Consumption in the afternoon and evening is going to impact your sleep. That includes not only coffee and energy drinks but also tea and chocolate.

Blue light from computer, television and phone screens tricks our body into thinking it is still bright out and delays the onset of melatonin. For my single friends, the late hours of the night can be a time of intense sexual arousal and intense loneliness. It is in these moments that the lure of dating apps and erotic websites reaches its zenith. Even if we manage to fall asleep just after a tiny amount of stimulus, the quality of our sleep will be compromised.

Alcohol is a depressant that makes it easier to pass out, but it affects the quality of sleep, especially if you drink too much or drink within a few hours of bedtime. I am well aware that advising young adults to limit alcohol intake before bedtime is impossible on weekends; for college students, it seems to be impossible any day of the week. But the facts don't lie. If you don't sleep, you don't prosper.

Dark Room

Ever been camping deep in the woods? Far away from civilization, where the glare of the nearest city's lights can't reach you? It's pitch-black, as I once learned with some indignity. Having to wake in the middle of the night to relieve myself of the copious amounts of hard cider I had consumed around the campfire, I hazily stumbled out of my tent into the darkness, fumbling with my belt buckle as I stepped off a small ledge and landed face down in the dirt below.

That's how black your room should be at night. No uncovered windows capturing streetlight, no computer screens on, no light coming from the hallway, not even little LED lights from charging plugs. Even with your eyes closed, the smallest light on your skin will disrupt the release of melatonin from your pineal gland and affect the deepness of your sleep. If you can still see your hands in front of your face, your room isn't dark enough.

Cool

Research says that the optimal sleeping temperature for most people is between 60 and 70 degrees. I would add a little nuance to this and say that the right temperature also has to do with the variance in heat between day and night. Our genes are programmed to sleep at temperatures cooler than those we experience during the day. You are probably at least subconsciously aware of this, setting your thermostat to a higher temperature in the summer than in the winter. In the African Savannah of our pre-clothing evolution, where we slept naked and without covers, nighttime temperatures fell to 68 during the dry season and only to 78 during the rainy season. Most of us wear at least some clothing while we sleep nowadays, use blankets, and have probably made some adaption to sleeping in the even colder climates of Europe and Asia or wherever we happen to be from. Between 60 and 70 degrees then seems a good bet. Just keep in mind as you program your thermostat to lower the temperature in the evening below your daytime level. A little nighttime chill will signal to your body that it is time to pass out.

Sanctuary

So much of sleep has to do with subconscious signals learned from habit. It is important that when you lie down your body takes this as a cue to pass out. Do not lay in bed to read, watch TV shows, or send emails. Your bed should be a place where only two activities occur. You know what they are. If you can dedicate your entire bedroom to nothing other than a good night's rest, even better. Keep your computer and television somewhere else in the house, and your bedroom a simple, uncluttered sanctuary that you enter and leave at regular times.

Stress

Once you have the external conditions for quality sleep all set up, the key is to never worry about sleep. Lying in bed, tossing and turning, feeding your mind negative thoughts like "I read that if I don't get eight hours of sleep I won't be able to function!" will only exacerbate your problem. The irony is that if you want great sleep, you can't worry about getting great sleep.

Help your mind to relax by taking it easy in the hours before bed. Avoid social media, particularly any news stories that might rile you up. Stay away from exciting television shows. And most important of all, avoid any interpersonal dispute. This is a time to read a book, meditate, listen to a podcast or cuddle with significant others. It is a time to wind down.

Get Out in Nature

Growing up in the suburbs, I dreamed of moving to a big city as an adult. A few times a year I would travel from Virginia to New York to visit family, always in complete awe the first moment a skyscraper came into view. In college, I chose to study abroad in the teeming metropolis of London. I craved the thrilling night life, the bustling streets, the ethnic diversity, the thousands and thousands of available women. I wanted to go to museums and concerts and art house cinemas, and to drink in crowded, boisterous pubs. Urban life was the life for me, I had no doubt.

All that would change in the fall of 2007, when at the age of 23 I went with a friend to see the movie "Into the Wild." It's the true story of Chris McCandless, a kid from the same part of Virginia as me, who took off into the wilderness in search of a more meaningful life than our drab, contemporary consumerist society could offer. The movie had a profound effect on me, and the very next day I planned to climb up Old Rag Mountain, one of the most famous hikes on the East Coast. The trail spirals a few thousand feet of elevation in only a couple of miles; the last hour of the hike is entirely rock scramble and a bit dangerous. Being out in nature, among the trees was invigorating. As my friend Logan and I reached the top, we rested on a rock, laid back and looked at the clear blue sky and the rolling Appalachian Mountains. Eagles soared above our heads. I felt a serenity and euphoria that I had not experienced in all the great cities I had visited.

On the way down, we were lost in conversation when we noticed a gargantuan pile of fresh feces in the middle of the trail. We wandered over to it, wondering what it might be, when we heard a rumbling in the bushes.

Bear.

When you come across a large animal capable of tearing you to shreds and having your liver for a snack, the first instinct of any normal person is to get the hell out of there. To my great surprise, my friend Logan grabbed his camera and took off towards the sounds of the thudding footsteps, rustling leaves, and growling noises. Not wanting to leave a friend alone to the whims of our omnivorous new acquaintance, I chased after Logan. We got within 20 feet or so and snapped a few photos. The bear looked at us, unfazed by our presence and rumbled off deeper into the wilderness. The whole experience gave me such an adrenaline rush that I practically galloped the rest of the way down the mountain.

That same night, I booked a flight to Hawaii, where my freshman college roommate lived as a surf instructor. I would spend a month there learning how to surf, jumping off cliffs, hiking through the tropical vegetation and nearly drowning while free-diving through underwater caves. It was as if a new world had opened up to me, a world that was at the same time far more relaxing and exciting than the life of the urban dweller I had fancied myself to be. A world that connected with some primal part of me. The world of Mother Nature.

Compare how different the modern urban environment is to the one in which our ancestors lived. 50,000 years ago you woke up in the morning, stepped out of your hut and rubbed your eyes, before taking in the sprawling view of the African savannah, the beaming sun and the sounds of exotic birds. You grabbed your bucket and headed to the local fresh water stream for a drink, perhaps stopping along the way to pluck a tasty fruit off a tree branch.

The hunter-gatherer is intimately familiar with the environment, sporting an encyclopedic knowledge of the local flora and fauna. To be effective hunters, men must learn the habits and patterns of hundreds of different species of animals. They learn to track the game by footprints, urine samples, and migration patterns. They become incredibly skilled at using their various hand-crafted weapons such as bows and arrows, blow-darts and spears.

For women, gathering food requires them to be knowledgeable about a wide swath of edible plant life, including roots, vegetables, tubers, seeds, nuts and fruit. They have to know when foods are ripe, what season they grew in, where to find them and how to extract them. Hunter-gatherers have to know how to make things from scratch -- like a house. They have to be able to predict the weather, treat wounds, and start a fire using sticks in under 30 seconds.

During my visit to the amazon, I was awed by the Waorani's mastery of the jungle. As we hiked through a dense thicket, we would stop at what appeared to be just another tree. But then a Waorani would slice open a tree branch to reveal delicious cool drinking water within. Minutes later, we gathered poison from the root of another tree, to place on the darts the tribe uses for hunting. Next, they cut off a few vines, and twirled them into rope to tie together a basket made of leaves from a nearby plant to carry all the items we collected. These guys were savants of the rainforest.

Studies of Nature

Psychologists have documented the numerous benefits of being surrounded by natural settings. A stroll through a natural setting, even if only for a few minutes, is relaxing, calms the mind, and allows one to replenish resources for attention. It lowers stress and improves one's mood. The Health Council of the Netherlands has found a positive link between living close to nature and human health. Hospital patients with a window view are more likely to survive than patients without. Those living in urban environments without parks and trees nearby are more likely to suffer from ill-health than those that live on greener boulevards. In one astonishing study, the simple act of placing plotted plants in view of workers at a factory reduced sick leave by 40 percent.

And it's not just our visual processes that are positively stimulated by nature. Our olfactory system inhales the phytochemicals released by plants; these aromas have an immensely positive effect on our mental and physical health by lowering stress hormones and reducing anxiety and pain, while increasing the effectiveness of our immune system. A study of Japanese businessmen who took a walk in the woods showed that the positive effects on their immune systems were still evident in tests done a month after their walk, and by a large amount!

Evidence suggests that not getting out into nature enough can lead to problems with obesity, attention-deficits and depression. It is not just the lack of natural flora that hurts us, being surrounded by the sounds of construction, traffic, honking horns, and the other cacophony of an urban environment has an additional negative effect on one's health and well-being. The scientific literature on the positive benefits of nature is vast and I could go on and on, but I think you get the point. Fill your abode with plants, have a window facing a towering oak, and get lost in the woods!

A Sense of the Divine

The Mbuti pygmies considered themselves the children of the forest, the forest being their Mother. HG's are known for having a spiritual connection with the world around them. This can often lead to forms of animism, giving anthropomorphic qualities to the trees, the landscape, the sun and moon. I am certainly not advocating any kind of spiritism, but neither do I have to in order to install a sense of wonder in Mother Nature. Good old science will do.

You are related to everything alive. You share a common ancestor not just with all other human beings, but with your pets, and even with the tree outside your window. Go back far enough and all our grandest of parents were the same cells in the ocean. Stand in the forest and all around you, from the towering trees to the ants crawling underneath your feet, are members of your extended family. Every second you are inhaling oxygen that flows into your blood and keeps your heart pumping. You quench your thirst with water gathered from the rain drops, and it's water that makes up 60 percent of your body. When you eat other life, be it plants or animals, that life is transformed into the very composite that is your flesh and bones. You are not separate from Mother Nature. You are a part of it, from the air you breathe to the minerals in your toenails.

Childhood Freedom

You are sitting around a campfire with your family, telling stories, laughing, having a good old time when your cute little toddler takes a wide-eyed interest in those warm, bright, red-and-orange flames leaping out from the fire pit. Perhaps she is wondering: "What is this thing that makes light? What would it be like to touch it?" She begins to crawl forward, inching closer and closer to the burning embers. You watch her calmly. She stretches out her hand, and there is still time to intervene, to pull her away, to scold her for putting herself in danger. But you don't. You watch motionlessly as her delicate fingers singe.

In HG culture, children are considered to have the same rights as anyone else, and those rights include not being told what to do -- even by their parents, even when their safety is at stake. This is just one of many dramatic differences between childhood now and the childhood we had for millions of years. These differences begin the very moment we are born.

A HG baby will be held to its mother's breast all day long. This was the norm long before we became *homo sapiens*. All our primate cousins maintain close contact between mother and newborn. Monkey and ape mothers will carry their young on their backs until they are ready to jump around on their own. Human mothers don't walk on all fours nor have a plethora of back hair (hopefully) for their offspring to cling to, so HG mothers will often wrap their babes in a blanket that they tie around their torso. A study of the !Kung found that their infants were held for 90 percent of the day, and when the mother wasn't able to hold the child it was always passed around to other members of the tribe. Travel writer J. Maarten Troost noted that the natives of the South Pacific islands absolutely loved babies. They held them continuously, stated that a baby should never cry, and that you should use your hands to mold the shape of the baby's skull into a nice round shape. When asked to do so for his own newborn, he politely declined. This constant contact has numerous benefits, including a sense of safety and comfort for the baby, increased skin-to-skin contact with the mother, as well as the mother's immediate presence should the baby begin to cry. HG babies rarely cry for more than 10-second bursts and in total cry far less often than the average baby born in modern society.

Being held at the mother's chest allows the child to breastfeed on demand. The baby will suckle multiple times per hour throughout the day. Infant-initiated nursing is practically impossible in our prudish societies, where, much to the chagrin of teenage boys, it is deemed inappropriate for a woman to walk around topless. The baby would have to remove the mother's shirt and bra on its own, a skill generally not mastered until at least high school. HG babies will even nurse when the mother is asleep, as the child will sleep in the same bed as the mother. The common fear today that a child and Mom shouldn't sleep in the same bed because she might roll over and smother the child is not a concern shared by HG moms. This could be because HG's sleep on harder surfaces than our cushy beds and are hence less likely to roll over in the night.

On average, HG moms breastfeed their children for three years. The frequency and duration with which they breastfeed likely activates what is known as "lactational amenorrhea," a physiological mechanism that inhibits ovulation and allows the mother to have unprotected sex without fear of getting pregnant for the duration of her breastfeeding. For this reason HG mothers usually don't have children closer than four years apart.

I am two years older than my brother, and when he was born, I was ecstatic. For a week. Then I realized that the flood of attention I was used to was now being focused on him instead. I expressed my concern to my mother in rather delicate terms: "Mom, it is time to get rid of Dylan. Throw him out the window, put him in the garbage. I don't care, just get rid of him." This sudden bifurcation in parent's emotional investment in their progeny was not something I was genetically programmed for. With good reason. An HG baby received the undivided attention of his parents until age four, when the next sibling was born. By then the HG child had a greater sense of autonomy; he also had other children in his tribe to play with.

This brings me to the greatest and most psychologically important difference between childhood in HG tribes and in modern life: education. Have you ever watched two lion cubs playing with each other? They wrestle around, jumping on each other's backs, lightly pawing and biting each other's necks. What looks like innocent goofing around is actually job training for the day when these cubs will grow into full-fledged predators of the Savannah and be expected to pounce on wild prey. In the animal world, there is no separation between play and education.

Despite the vast expanse of knowledge children in hunter-gatherer tribes had to acquire, none of this learning took place in a classroom setting. All the skills they needed to master were directly connected to their future profession as *savants* of the natural world. Children acquired this mastery not from intense study, but by the same method other mammals in the animal kingdom learn -- imitation and play. And play they did, from the time they woke up until the time they went to sleep.

Parents in contemporary HG societies do not express any worry about their child's education. They don't plan any curricula nor do they teach a child anything unless directly asked. The kids learn completely on their own and through their own initiative. Children are considered autonomous individuals who are free to do whatever they want nearly all day long. The children run off into the forest with their little spears and bows and arrows, where they hunt small game, and pretend to wage mock wars. They build play huts, smaller versions of the real huts they live in, and put on theatrical performances, acting out how they have observed adults interacting. They learn to build tools such as arrowheads, rope and rafts mostly with the help of older children, who teach them all this in the process of playing a game.

Not until late adolescence are these children considered old enough to do work. And when it is time for them to contribute to the group, they do so willingly. Children in primitive societies are raised with a hands-off approach to a degree that modern parents would consider madness. It is common in a HG village to see a two-year-old swinging around a machete. This is so unusual I have a hard time believing it, but it is completely unnatural for a parent to tell their child what to do, even when saying something could keep the child from great harm. Despite our fears that without our guidance children will grow up to be maniacs, this simply doesn't happen in HG society. As anthropologist Elizabeth Marshall Thomas wrote of the Ju/'hoansi tribe:

Ju/'hoan children very rarely cried, probably because they had little to cry about. No child was ever yelled at or slapped or physically punished, and few were even scolded. Most never heard a discouraging word until they were approaching adolescence, and even then the reprimand, if it really was a reprimand, was delivered in a soft voice... We are sometimes told that children who are treated so kindly become spoiled, but this is because those who hold that opinion have no idea how successful such measures can be. Free from frustration or anxiety, sunny and cooperative, the children were every parent's dream. No culture can ever have raised better, more intelligent, more likable, more confident children.

Jared Diamond, reflecting on the 49 years that he had known tribes in the New Guinea Highlands and reviewing what other westerners had written about HG children, had this to say:

A recurring theme is that other Westerners and I are struck by the emotional security, self-confidence, curiosity, and autonomy of members of small-scale societies, not only as adults, but already as children. We see that people in small-scale societies spend far more time talking to each other than we do...we are struck by the precocious development of the social skills in their children...the adolescent identity crisis that plagues American teenagers isn't an issue for hunter-gatherer children.

I would add to Diamond's assessment that it is not just a case of the things they do that we don't, but the numerous stresses HGs don't have to endure that our kids do. As I remember my childhood, I think back to the absolute dread that accompanied a Monday morning, waking up to the alarm clock far earlier than I wished and having to drag myself to the bus stop. The hours spent daydreaming as I struggled to tune into the endless drone of a lecture. Gazing out the window and checking the clock, counting down the hours to when the final school bell rang and I was free to go home and play with the neighborhood kids. There is a reason boys roughhouse, run around and otherwise can't sit still in classrooms, or that girls are constantly chatting and discretely texting each other while they are supposed to be studying; a reason that children of all ages struggle to do homework, dislike doing chores and are otherwise disobedient to their parents' demands. Kids are not genetically programmed to sit in classrooms, learn material that they see as unrelated to things they want to do, or to have their freedom to do what they want, when they want, infringed upon in anyway.

So what can we do? Clearly we are not going to take our children out of school, and stop teaching them reading, writing and arithmetic. And if we let them do what they want when they want, they might not ever put down that iPad. The world children grow up in today is so vastly different from the one of our ancestors, it might seem that all is hopeless. But there are a few things we can do to help our kids grow up with more confidence and autonomy. Number one is stop being so overprotective.

In my work as a brain trainer, I have a lot of clients who are children and I get to see how their mothers interact with them and inevitably, what kind of personalities the kids have. One child, a fifth grader, had to leave the office to go to the hallway bathroom, a mere ten feet away. His mother, immediately worrying about him, followed him to the bathroom and waited outside until he came back out. She meant well, but her overbearing coddling was the exact opposite of what her son needed to become a self-confident, autonomous individual. In training, he was a little crybaby. Tears would flow the moment he had to do anything remotely challenging. Kids learn confidence by overcoming obstacles, especially ones that they perceive as dangerous. Let them roughhouse and go exploring deep in the woods. Don't force them to check in every five minutes to make sure they are OK. Let them run off and come back when they feel like it.

In other words: Stop worrying about them. Psychologists understand that worrying is a learned behavior and that anxious parents teach their children to worry. They view the world as a dangerous place, and this paradigm is then passed on to the child. A child is up to seven times more likely to develop an anxiety disorder if a parent has an anxiety problem himself. While you might think that your worrying is pro-actively keeping them safe, the reality is this: Teaching the child to worry and feel that the world is a scary place is only going to lead to raising a neurotic kid. Neuroticism is the death knell of well-being, having effects both on the child's happiness and on the child's physical health, as we know that stress can break down the proper functioning of a child's immune system. Of course, you can still teach a child not to get into cars with strangers, and to look both ways when crossing the street. But you can do this with a calm rationality. Embrace the paradox that to raise a happy and healthy child, you can't worry about your child's health and happiness.

Beautiful Faces

What makes for an attractive face? For men, it is symmetrical features, a chiseled jawline, prominent cheekbones. A pretty woman has a face that is broad, symmetrical, with high cheekbones, a small nose, and wide-set eyes. Look at yourself in the mirror just as you have done thousands of times before and examine the dimensions of your face. How closely do they align with the standard of beauty? Has your attractiveness improved or waned over time? How did you end up with the face that you have now? Was it destined since the moment of your birth, or has your behavior and environment shaped the way your face has grown?

We all know that diet, posture and exercise can radically change the attractiveness of our bodies, but few realize that diet, posture and exercise also affect the attractiveness of the most visible appendage we have: the one positioned directly above the neck. According to Dr. Mike Mew, only a small percentage of people in modern society have properly formed faces: the Clint Eastwoods and Kate Mosses of the world. The other 95 percent of us poor schmucks have faces that range from slightly off-kilter to grossly hideous.

This is the exact opposite of ancestral society, where nearly everyone was good-looking. Or at the very least, they thought so. In a study done on the Maasai by psychologist

Robert Biswas-Diener, every single one of the 120 people he asked said that they were "completely satisfied with their physical appearance." Is there anyone you know in modern society who would make that claim?

When I visited the Waorani tribe of the Amazon, one of the first things that struck me about their appearance was their teeth. Were they brown, missing and crooked as you would expect a person who had never visited a dentist? No. They were perfect, not only in their color, but in their alignment. The best Beverly Hills orthodontist could not have done better. The Mew family agrees.

Mew is a third-generation orthodontist, and it was his father who traveled to the jungle of Kenya to find tribal people and study their teeth. What did he find? Not only did the majority have straight teeth, despite having never seen an orthodontist, but they also had their wisdom teeth intact. And, surprisingly, they even had 10mm of extra room behind their wisdom teeth.

When I got my wisdom teeth taken out as a late teenager, I was perplexed by the explanation that my mouth wasn't naturally big enough to fit all my teeth. Why then did I have these extraneous teeth in the first place? Were they really a useless relic of our Cro-Magnon past? No, as a group of dentists and orthodontists have been finding out. The problem is that our faces have become unnaturally long and thin, leaving our jaws too narrow for our teeth to grow into place properly. This results in malocclusion, the scientific term for crooked teeth.

In the 1960s, a group of anthropologists studied a hunter-gatherer tribe in Brazil known as the Xavante. Ninety-five percent of the Xavante had perfect smiles. Their teeth were aligned, their arches wide, while the other five percent had only slightly imperfect smiles, with just some mild crowding of the front teeth. Not a single

Xavante had an overbite or underbite. A neighboring tribe, living at a government outpost and eating more processed foods, showed a far greater prevalence of malocclusion. In his extensive studies of the dental health of tribal societies around the world, Dr. Weston Price noticed the same thing: Every time a group shifted from their traditional diet to a modern one, their rates of malocclusion skyrocketed. And it's not just present-day traditional societies that show stunning dental health. Our ancestors did even better! Dr. Price studied hundreds of prehistoric skulls found in burial grounds of ancient South American, Australian and New Zealand peoples. None of the skulls showed evidence of tooth decay, malocclusion or dental arch deformity.

But the descendants of these people who adopted modern culture all show high incidences of these failings. Why does this happen? What is going on in modern society that is causing our faces to become deformed, and hence give us bad teeth? It's always good to start at the beginning, and we might think that this means in the womb, where our skulls begin to develop a bit after the first month of pregnancy. Of course, the nutrients we get from our mother's diet are essential for ensuring that we have proper facial growth during this time period, but our time in the womb can also be affected by what our moms ate in the months prior to our being conceived. According to neurobiologist Stephan Guyanet, Vitamins A, folic acid, D, and Vitamin K2 are stored in the body for a long period of time. He notes that many tribal societies would prepare mothers for pregnancy by ensuring that they stocked up on green, leafy vegetables and meat.

The shaping of the face and jaw mostly takes place between birth and age four. Hence, the majority of facial deformities and malocclusion will be established during this period. A key aspect of attractiveness -- facial symmetry --

can be derailed due to childhood malnutrition, illness, exposure to tobacco smoke and pollutants. Studies have shown that the longer a woman breastfeeds her child, the more nourished he or she will be, and the less likely the child will develop malocclusion. On top of that, bottle-feeding, pacifier use and thumb-sucking all dramatically increase the rate of malocclusion. The muscles a baby uses while breastfeeding, as well as chewing solid food when it is able to, will lead to the foundation of strong, healthy jaws.

We all know that exercise is important for the health and growth of our muscles and bones. So why would we think it would be any different for the muscles and bones in our face? The single best predictor of malocclusion is whether the person ate soft or tough foods. Those that ate soft foods early in life, have jaws that developed improperly. Our hunter-gatherer ancestors ate a variety of tough, unprocessed foods that gave their jaws a real workout. Biting into a steak and chewing on the fat is harder than eating pasta. And they didn't just use their teeth for eating, but also for holding items while their hands were occupied, or working with leather and fibers. And while your orthodontist can fix your teeth, your orthodontist doesn't do anything about the underlying problem: your deformed mug. When we don't have nice, strong jaws, a cascade of other problems ensue. Without a sufficiently large jaw, our tongues have less room in our throat, and this interferes with breathing.

We compensate for this by opening our mouths to let in more air. When we breath through our mouths the tongue isn't resting in its proper position on the roof of the mouth. Without the pressure from the tongue on the roof of the mouth, the top of your mouth will cave in, dropping downwards and thinning, leaving less horizontal room for all your teeth. *Hello, malocclusion.* Also with less airway space, hello, snoring, hello, sleep apnea, hello, angry spouse.

What can we do to stop all this? Listen to your grandmother. Develop good posture. Stand up straight and make sure that your neck isn't leaning too far forward, that your ears align with your shoulders. This opens up your chest and throat for proper breathing through the nostrils, as you keep your mouth shut and your teeth touching, or nearly so. Dr. Mew recommends the mantra, "Teeth together, lips together, tongue at the roof of your mouth."

And eat your carrots.

Why Can't I See?

Sometime during my teenage years, I began waving to people I didn't know. "Have we met?" asks the perplexed stranger. "Oh sorry, I thought you were my friend." At the time, I blamed my poor vision on genetics. After all, my father had similar vision. My brother wore contacts, so it all just made sense. I pondered how it was that the gene for bad eyesight had not been weeded out of existence thousands of years ago. Corrective lenses haven't been around that long, so how did our ancestors survive when they couldn't even see what was right in front of them? By the time they reached adolescence, they would have run into a tree or mistaken a venomous snake for a twig and been hastily swept out of the gene pool.

The theory that myopia (near-sightedness) was due to bad genetics was the prominent view among scientists in the middle of the 20th century, despite evidence of the fantastic vision of hunter-gatherers. The 1937 study "The ocular refractive state of the Palae-Negroids in Gabon, French Equatorial Africa" (that title wouldn't fly today) showed that of the 2,364 members of the various hunter-gatherer tribes in the region studied, only 13 total eyes had any incidence of myopia. Far away on the other side of the Atlantic, tribes of Amazonian Indians reported only two percent of their population to be near-sighted. Similarly, a

1954 study done on the Eskimos of Greenland found evidence of myopia in only 1.2% of the population. Still, the scientists who thought vision was mostly genetic stuck to their guns. It was felt that there would have been tremendous evolutionary pressure on HG groups to develop great eyesight, something lost to the modern world. But then evidence started mounting, evidence that just could not be explained away by anything other than environmental factors.

Another group of Eskimos from Alaska was studied. The older members of the group who had lived a HG existence had a rate of myopia of only 1.5 percent. Their children, acclimated to a modern existence and the first members of the tribe to grow up attending school, weren't so lucky. Unlike their elders, they spent their days inside reading books. The rate of myopia for the new generation? 51 percent.

The genetic hypothesis further crumbled as a wave of myopia swept the modern world. Nowhere has the effect been more pronounced than in East Asia, where rates of myopia amongst 20-year-olds have risen from the 10-to-20 percent range to upwards of 90 percent in the last 50 years. Clearly, this problem has an environmental component. But what is the cause?

Scientists began to look for correlations that could explain this epidemic of myopia. What were kids doing differently now than they were a century ago? There seemed to be an obvious answer. Children were spending a lot more time in front of computer screens, playing video games, and doing obscene amounts of studying and homework -- especially those brainy Asian kids. Could all this looking at objects up close be the cause of near-sightedness?

Research experiments were done that tracked kids, their habits, and their rate of myopia. What they found was surprising. The kids whose eyesight remained intact did not vary much in terms of the amount of time that they read or used a computer. Sure, it mattered some, but it wasn't telling the whole story. There was another variable, however, that did prove to be the major player. The kids who were consistently least affected by near-sightedness, across studies, across continents, were the ones who spent more time playing outdoors.

Being outside has at least two protective functions against losing your eyesight: greater viewing distances and exposure to bright light. Spending more time gazing off into the distance seems to have an obvious benefit if your goal is to further the distance you can see. But how does being exposed to bright light help? The physical cause of myopia is a lengthening of the eyeball, which was a bit of a mystery for researchers. How does decreasing your exposure to bright light cause your eyeball to lengthen? The leading hypothesis is that humans naturally have a diurnal rhythm, sending a spike of dopamine to the retina when exposed to daylight. If our eyes don't get this injection of dopamine, your eye development gets out of whack and the eyeball will lengthen. Light entering the eye gets refracted, and the image won't reach all the way to the retina, which is located at the back of the eyeball. Hence, near-sightedness.

The allure of the indoor universe with the advent of computers, video games, and television is strong. But even a well-lit room provides light levels of only about 500 lux. The amount needed for myopia prevention is at least 10,000 lux for three hours a day. This is the kind of bright light that our ancestors bathed in on sunny afternoons.

No Soap, No Shampoo

Ah, the wonderful Halloween. A night where women are free to dress in scanty, seductive outfits without the fear of being labeled sluts. Me? I was braving the cold in a pair of tighty whities as part of my Tom Cruise in Risky Business outfit. I knew it would garner attention, but as I would later find out, it wasn't my top weapon of attraction for the night.

A dozen of my friends and I went out clubbing in the city, dancing and drinking assorted libations when my buddy Steve met a provocative woman dressed in a titillating school girl's costume. Her friend, dressed as a ballerina, was cute too, and I chatted her up. Vodka infused-drinks were bought and sensual dancing ensued. The girls took a liking to us and followed us from one club to the next. We were in. Steve was going to hook up with the school girl and me with the ballerina. But then something interesting happened. As we posed for a group picture the school girl got close to me, a switch was flipped and for the rest of the night she stuck to me like glue, dancing with me, sitting on my lap, holding my hand. She jumped ship from Steve to me. At first I put off her advances, but when I realized Steve didn't care which of these two girls he hooked up with, I turned to the ballerina and said, "Go be with Steve, he likes you." Realizing that I preferred her friend, she acquiesced. The two of them got along swimmingly, and the school girl was all mine.

Later that night, basking in a post-coital glow, I turned to the school girl and asked her why the change of heart. She seemed to be really into Steve, so why did she suddenly jump all over me? "When I got really close to you for that group picture, I smelled you," she said. "And you smelled hot! Like a man. And Steve, he just smelled like..like..nothing. You smelled so good I was overcome with the most intense compulsion to fellate you." I laughed and told her my dirty little secret. I hadn't used soap or shampoo in the shower in months.

My no-soap, no-shampoo lifestyle began with a thought experiment. There are billions of species of social animals on this planet. They live together in bands, roll around in the dirt, swim in rivers, run, exercise, sweat and make love with each other, all without ever using bars of oily fats derived from animal innards, mixed with hard-to-pronounce-metals in order to cleanse themselves. Yet our species is somehow different.

Ask a random person on the street what would happen if the entire population neglected to wash with soap and you would probably get an answer along the lines of: "The smell would be unbearable. It would be like France, but way worse." Yet for hundreds of thousands of years, *homo sapiens* lived with each other, slept in the same huts, embraced, hugged, cuddled and ate meals together long before the invention of soap. Soap only was invented a few thousand years ago and only became widely used in the past few centuries. Are we to believe that for all that time people were walking around each other with their noses clenched?

Skeptic: But wait just a minute; if I go a couple days without showering, I smell. I mean I *really* smell. This isn't just in my imagination.

A: Oh, I'm sure you do. The problem is that the constant soaping and lathering have stripped your body of its natural cleansing mechanisms and healthy bacteria. Your body produces an oil called sebum which has the beneficial effects of killing germs, protecting against the sun, and moisturizing the skin. It also has vital anti-inflammatory properties, and is a delivery system for antioxidants and pheromones, the chemicals that attract you to the opposite sex. Every time you wash with soap, you not only wash off any grime you have accumulated; you also wash off your natural, healthy oils. You spend countless dollars trying to replace their functions with moisturizers, sunscreen, perfumes, and other products, when all you had to do was not wash it away in the first place.

Your hair and skin also serve as a home to a living microbiome of miniature organisms. These bacteria and fungi play a beneficial role to your overall health because of their symbiotic relationship. The positive effects of good bacteria include producing their own antibiotics that kill off bad bacteria, fight off skin infections and produce their own fragrance. It could take your body weeks to fully recover the microbiome and restore your skin to its natural sebum production after using soap. The reason you smell after not bathing for a few days is because during your last washing, you stripped away your body's natural oils and bacteria and now have nothing to replace it with. After some time, when your body returns to normal functioning, your smell will no longer be putrid, but will be rather pleasant -- even the nether regions, which I have been complimented on as giving off the aroma of a berry lollipop. And this isn't just for men who want to be manly; it works for the fairer sex as well.

Love at first smell. That is how I would describe one particular romance I had with a flower child from San Francisco. What was her secret? Was it a special perfume? I doubt it, for chemical fragrances are often too pungent for my tastes. A special blend of pheromones that matched perfectly to the aesthetic preference of my nostrils? Perhaps. But I believe the answer was given as we walked hand in hand through a tree-lined path in the orange hue of autumn. Her hair blowing in the breeze, me floating in the air like Pepe Le Peu. Why did she smell so good? "I don't use soap in the shower," she said.

During my puerile, naive years, those first 28 years of my life when I wasted precious minutes of my morning plastering globs of sodium laureth sulfate and other chemicals on my head, I had dry, unmanageable hair that became a greasy mess if I went so long as 24 hours without using shampoo. I imagined at the time that if I were to suspend shampoo use indefinitely my hair would grow exponentially greasier and malodorous. How silly I was.

When I decided to purge shampoo from my life, I did my research and planned for the future. I knew that in response to the chemicals that strip away the natural oils on your head, the scalp will produce excess sebum. Hence the greasy look a mere 24 hours after using shampoo. After decades of daily washing, my scalp was accustomed to producing enormous amounts of sebum everyday, and this would not change overnight. I was going to have to go through an adjustment period where my hair, which was pretty long at the time, would look as if I had bathed it in mayonnaise. And to be honest, for the next two months my hair was pretty gross. But then my scalp turned a corner and shut off the too-much-sebum faucet and my hair became less and less greasy, finally resting in a place where my hair has a natural shine. It is easily manageable, and I don't need any styling products. I do have days where my hair does get greasy without a good rinse, but not nearly as bad as it would be if I had been using shampoo and then went some time without.

Once you make it past the initial recovery phase of the no-soap, no-shampoo lifestyle you will be shocked that almost no one notices. Here you are, engaging in hygiene practices that most people would consider repugnant, and yet they remain completely unawares. Give the no-soap, no-shampoo lifestyle a chance. As to whether you should divulge your secret to the average close-minded commoner, I'll leave that decision up to you.

Are Toilets Bad For You?

I awoke to the sounds of birds and crickets as the morning sunbeams crept through the canvas fibers of my sleeping tent. I unzipped the semicircular opening and stepped out to embrace the rarified air. I yawned and stretched out to my full height, taking in the endless sea of conifers and mountain ridges spread out in every direction from our 8500-foot perch overlooking Lake Tahoe. The radiance of the moment was only interrupted by the rumbling in my belly caused by last night's canned dinner. But I did not despair, for these grumblings portended a new opportunity! A chance to conquer a necessary right of passage into adulthood, to help put an end to an adolescence that had overstayed its welcome, dogging me well into my mid-twenties. To engage in a ritual that connected a primal part of my being to all other forms of life on the planet.

It was time to take a shit in the woods.

Once upon a time, this was the only way to relieve yourself, before the invention of the outhouse, and eventually the home toilet. We now hide ourselves alone in a room, sit down and empty our bowels in total seclusion. We flush away the remnants, never to be seen again. This is the dignified way to do it, right? Not like a pathetic animal, depositing our turds on the cold, hard ground. Alas, friends, never underestimate the mental insularity that comes with the pretense of being "civilized".

As I walked away from the tent in search of a pristine spot to dispose of my droppings, I began to grow a bit trepidatious. My callowness in the art of defecating *au natural* began to froth up in the form of apprehensive thoughts. What about technique? I simply squat all the way down, right? Will my legs get tired? What if someone sees me? True, I had walked deep into the woods to make sure no one would come near, but there was still a possibility that someone could walk past. How awkward would that be? Here I am squatting down, taking a dump, and someone could just walk right past me out here in the open wilderness!

Fuck it. I'm going for it. I squatted all the way down. My fear that this might be a long bowel movement quickly passed. With the angle of my body in the full squat position, it came out quick, fast, clean. Never in my life had I experienced such a sublime, effortless expulsion of feces.

I looked around the mountain top where I was squatting. The beautiful sunshine lit my face, the songs of the birds danced on the waves of crisp air. I felt free. Then it hit me. A thought so profound I had to tell someone at once! I rushed back to the campsite where my friends were. They were packing for the day's hike. I interrupted them.

"It's all a scam!" I yelled.

"What? What are you talking about? What's a scam?"

"Toilets."

That's right, ladies and gentleman, toilets are bad for you.

Here in the western world we think of the elevated toilet, where we sit with our legs at a 90-degree angle, as the only way to take a dump. It may shock you to know that most of the world uses the squat toilet instead. A squat toilet is basically a hole in the ground that will also flush in the same manner as our toilets. It is not only more natural, but a quicker and healthier way to take a shit. The evidence is backed by science. Honest.

In a paper published in the *Journal of Medical Hypotheses* hilariously entitled "Cardio-vascular Events at Defecation: Are They Unavoidable?" the angle of the sitting position is said to be obstructive, causing the defecating human to try and force out the excrement with multiple excessive pushes that tax the cardiovascular system. While it may seem ridiculous, dying of a heart attack on the toilet is a common cause of death amongst the elderly. Dr. Berko Sikirov, the leading researcher in this field (his mother is very proud), says that the sitting position is three times more strenuous than the squatting position and can lead to hemorrhoids and colonic diverticulosis.

For those of us in relatively good health, there are other benefits of the squatting position. Primarily, it is faster and smoother. Dr. Sikirov did another study where he timed how long people defecated in both the squatting and sitting position. By his calculations, the average time squatters spent shitting was 51 seconds, the fastest being a 21-year-old female who over a six-shit sample averaged only five seconds per dump. Incredible.

For those sitting at the average toilet height, it was two-minutes-and-10 seconds. Anecdotally, I can confirm these results and add that the most time added on is in the act of cleaning up. When squatting, the feces comes out so smoothly that you hardly have to wipe!

If you have grown up in the western world and don't feel like remodeling your entire bathroom to put in a squat toilet, it's okay. There are other options. There are awkward contraptions that you can place around your toilet, that you can stand on and squat. But the most practical option is to get a stool that you put your feet on. A popular brand is called Squatty Potty. While you won't be able to get into the full squat position, it is still better than your normal sitting posture. From personal experience, let me assure you that this simple device will make the process of emptying your bowels more enjoyable, it is far healthier, and it will save you lots of time. Then go ahead and get a cheap bidet that attaches to your toilet so that you never have to wipe again. You can thank me for afterwards for changing your life.

Work, A Modern Invention

In the Amazon jungle I awoke to the sounds of birds singing and the river flowing. Not in any great hurry, I stretched out in the sun and chatted leisurely with my native guides, Fausto and Orlando. They were members of the Kichwa tribe, a native Amazonian group who fought a vicious war with the Waorani only a generation ago. But things had settled down in the past few years and I had hired them to take me to the visit the Waorani. They asked me what I wanted to do most during the time I would spend living with the Waorani, and I could only think of one answer. I wanted to hunt.

Fabiano showed up around nine a.m. wearing his traditional Waorani get-up: a simple skirt made out of bark, plus a new pair of green rain boots. After 25 years of going barefoot, his third poisonous snakebite only a week earlier had finally convinced him of the benefits of donning protective foot-wear. Over his right shoulder he had an eight-foot blowgun. Slung over his left shoulder was a quiver of darts, coated at the tips with poison.

He handed me a spear. At first I thought it was just for me to examine, so I looked it over and handed it back to him. No, he said, it was for me to use during the hunt. How else was I supposed to kill a charging boar?

Fausto and Orlando would get spears as well, and the four of us trekked off into the jungle. Fabiono's knowledge of the flora and fauna was mind-boggling. We stopped at something he calls the Toucan plant, because by ripping off one of its leaves, licking it, and rolling it up, you can bring it to your lips and make a whistling sound that imitates the mating call of a toucan.

We continued our walk through the thicket of giant leaves, spider webs, and thorny underbrush. We were moving slowly, quietly, not wanting to alert any potential game to our presence. Suddenly, Fabiano waved for us to stop dead in our tracks. Peccaries! That is, Amazonian boar. We could hear them off in the distance, but they were down a steep incline from us, so we would have to approach carefully. He began to load his blowgun. I looked over at Orlando, seemingly uninterested in the peccaries, his eyes fixed on the canopy above us. "Monkeys," he whispered. Fabiano turned with his blowgun and aimed towards the sky. Too late, they spotted us, and those quick little guys took off, hopping from branch to branch and were soon out of sight.

For some reason, Fabiano gave up on trying to catch the peccaries as well, and instead turned his attention towards hunting toucans. There were plenty of them around; the only problem was they were sitting on branches at least 150 feet above the ground. Not an easy shot, even for a blowgun specialist like Fabiano. He shot at five different birds, but each time the dart whizzed inches away from its target, never quite hitting the mark.

Unable to shoot or spear any wild animals, we turned our attention to gathering fruits. Orlando noticed a bunch of purple fruits that had fallen from a tree onto the ground. Orlando then scaled the tree, which had no branches and was only about six inches in diameter, until he was at least

50 feet up. He then shook the branches containing the fruit, and soon hundreds of the purple "nuts" fell to the ground. We ate a few on the spot. But the real treasure would be later on when we mashed them up and turned these fruits into a chocolate-flavored drink. Lacking a receptacle to carry them in, Fabiano grabbed a nearby plant and in under a minute folded the leaves together to construct a makeshift basket.

With fruits in hand, we still needed to acquire some protein. Fabiano saw what looked to me like any ordinary branch of a plant. He sliced it open to reveal a colony of lemon ants. "Eat," he said. "Tastes good. Like lemon. Once my father and I were lost in the jungle for days, and all we had to go on were eating these ants." I scooped up a handful and chucked them in my mouth. They really did taste like lemon.

But these tasty ants weren't going to be enough to feed us or his family. So we went to the river to catch some fish. The Waorani don't use a rod and reel to fish. Fabiano offered two reasons for this. The first was sensible: The fish in this river don't have teeth capable of latching on to the bait. The second, to my scientific ears, sounded completely absurd. To catch one of these fish with a rod and reel was a bad omen. If you did so, your family would die. Sensing my incredulity, Fabiano told a story of a girl who once caught a fish in this river with a rod and reel. A month later her father died.

With conventional fishing gear declared off-limits, Fabiano used a net to quarter off part of the river. If a fish swam into the net, he grabbed it with his bare hands and tossed it onto the shore where it would suffocate. Smaller fish were simply caught by placing our hands under rocks where they might be hiding. To kill them, we bit them in the head before they could squirm free from our fingers. By mid-afternoon, we returned to the village with a basket brimming with fish and fruits.

I asked Fabiano how often he goes hunting or fishing. He said only once every couple of weeks. Other times, he eats the yuca and plantains that the women gather. Or another male in the tribe will catch a monkey to share with everyone. If hunting is considered work, Fabiano hardly worked at all.

While the public perception is that our foraging ancestors slaved and toiled year round in search of sustenance, the truth is they were the most leisurely people on the face of the earth. They didn't have jobs. There were no lawyers, accountants or factory workers back then. All that was needed to live the good life was to go out into the wilderness and get food. And that didn't take long.

Studies of the !Kung tribe in Botswana reveal that they spent between 12 and 19 hours a week collecting the food they needed. The Hadza of Tanzania did it in about 14 hours. Other tribes in Africa and the Amazon spent similar amounts of time in search of food. Sure, they had to do other things -- making baskets, collecting firewood, preparing food, etc. -- but modern people have to do our numerous chores every day on top of the 40 hours a week we spend trapped in our offices. The human animal is simply not equipped, either physically or mentally, to work more than a few hours a day.

The Protestant work ethic is not going to lead to happiness. It is going to kill you. In construction and transportation jobs, accidental death occurs frequently. For an office job, a period of long stressful hours is known to cause heart failure. In Japan they have a term called "karoshi," which means death from overwork. In the United States, we don't classify people whose hearts stop during overtime work as having died from work-related stress. But it does happen to us, too. And if we aren't dying from working 30 hours in a row with no breaks, our careers are killing us slowly. Long working hours correlate with prolonged sitting, increased psychological stress, lack of leisure time, lack of family contact, and inadequate time to exercise and eat healthy meals. All of this leads to poor health and premature death, not to mention anxiety and depression.

Despite this grim outlook, there is a substantial proportion of the population who would love to have these First World problems. They suffer from the far more hazardous condition of not being employed at all. According to a study done at Harvard, laid-off workers were 83 percent more likely to develop a stress-related illness than the employed. In Finland, a study showed that people who had been unemployed at least twice in their lives were nearly three times more likely to die an early death. Even the fear of losing one's job has been shown to raise one's cholesterol levels. This dire fear of unemployment was not something our ancestors had to face.

It's not just the workload or lack of work that cause all our contemporary health problems. Another trouble in the twenty-first century is that most of us feel a lack of meaning and purpose at our jobs. Studies have shown that people who have a direction and purpose live longer. The problem with finding meaning and purpose in life in modern society is twofold:

1) We have so many choices about what to do for work that we are too paralyzed to make choices.

2) The activities that we engage in are hardly recognized by our body as contributing to our survival and replicating value (SRV).

Our HG ancestors did not suffer from career-related stress. They didn't have to decide whether they wanted to be insurance salesmen, writers, accountants, or strippers. They didn't have to decide whether to take the high-paying job at the law firm or work for the non-profit at a vastly reduced salary. While we often think having a number of options to choose from is a good thing, psychologists have now shown that when faced with too many choices, people get stressed out.

Gonga, a living member of the Hadzabe tribe in Africa, had this to say about who he was. "Only when I am sleeping, I am not a hunter. I am a hunter all the time I am awake. That is what I am and who I am. I kill animals for meat."

Hunting (or gathering for women) is the original career choice for humans. There is a direct connection between the necessity to hunt and the end goal of eating food. With any other job in modern society, the degrees of separation from the ultimate objective take away from its meaning. This is problem number 2. The reward system to motivate us towards actions that are beneficial for our survival and replication value evolved during our days in the African Savannah. Work in the modern world is too far removed from what your body knows to be beneficial for your SRV.

Imagine you are a bank teller. You help people withdraw and deposit money from their accounts. You sit behind a counter, press buttons on a computer. You don't particularly enjoy this job; you do it so you can get paid, so that you have money to buy food. Being a bank teller raises your SRV, but in such a way that your body hardly recognizes it.

Working to earn money to go to the store to buy food is not as visceral an objective as hunting. I am hungry, I must find an animal, engage in a life or death battle with it, kill it, and then eat it. I'll bring it home to the tribe, where the women will be grateful for the danger I have put myself in to bring them this delicious source of protein, and they will sleep with me for it.

We are all searching for a job, a purpose that replicates hunting and gathering. We just aren't aware of it. People often say things like "I want to do something meaningful." Jobs that are often described as meaningful are those that help other people, like being a nurse, a teacher, an environmental scientist or running a non-profit organization.

Think about it, though: What could be more meaningful than feeding your entire hungry tribe? Your family and friends who you have known your entire life? To put food in your hungry belly and theirs? There cannot be any job more meaningful than hunting or gathering. Imagine a conversation about finding purpose and meaning in life conducted between you and Gonga.

You: "I want to do something exciting"

Gonga: "What could be more exciting than fighting a wild animal in a game of life or death?"

You: "I want to do something that is intellectually challenging."

Gonga: "Have you ever learned how to track game? Can you tell where that antelope will be by the footprint he left in the dirt?"

You: "I can't handle the monotony of my job!"

Gonga: "Today, we hike into the forests for wild boar. In a few days we will fish by the river. And then we will set traps to catch birds."

You: "I don't like my co-workers or my boss."

Gonga: "I hunt with my friends and cousins. My wife gathers food with her sisters and friends. They will laugh and gossip."

You: "I spend most of my day sitting in front of a computer screen, ruining my eyes, and getting fat."

Gonga: "I hike every day in beautiful nature. I stare into the distant horizon. I bathe in the sun's rays. I am lean and muscular."

You: "Work is stressful. I want to do something different, but I can't risk losing my paycheck."

Gonga: "I love to hunt. I don't even have a word in my vocabulary that corresponds to *work*."

Sex, Love, and Relationships

When men from the Aka Pygmy tribe in Africa told anthropologists Barry and Bonnie Hewlett how often they had sex, the scientists laughed it off. It was just men boasting. No way these guys were having sex three to four times a night! But then the anthropologists went and asked the women, and it turned out that the men weren't exaggerating at all. The Aka women are so ravenous that their male partners live with the fear that they must inseminate these women multiple times before the sun rises, lest the women leave them. To protect against this, the men gathered a natural Viagra from the bark of a local tree called Bulomba, which acts as a sexual stimulant.

The Aka experience is a far cry from the modern stereotype humorously examined in "Annie Hall." Speaking to a therapist, Woody Allen's character is asked how often he has sex. "Hardly ever. Maybe three times a week." His girlfriend, played by Diane Keaton, is shown on the split screen answering the same question from *her* therapist, "Constantly, I'd say three times a week."

If that couple had stayed together, chances are the frequency of their copulations would have dropped even further. Recent research suggests the average married couple has sex about once a week. One out of every five married couples has sex less than ten times a year, and somewhere between 25 percent of men and 40 percent of women complain of having no sex drive at all. How did it get this way?

A Modern Love Story

Jack and Jill meet. She thinks he's cute. He can't wait to sleep with her. They go on a date to assess common interests. They like the same obscure indie band, they both love Barcelona, she loves rollerblading, he pretends he does, too. More drinks are ordered, hair is fiddled with, hands are touched, an Uber is called, and they are back at his place to "watch a movie". A few minutes of spastic humping ensue, and he orgasms. She pretends that she does too.

Remarkably, she would like to see him again. They go for a hike, tell stories about their childhood, make love. There are double dates with friends, dance lessons, and awkward encounters with each other's parents. They can't believe how lucky they are to have found each other. That one true person of all the billions on earth that brings the soul to completion. There are roses, and poems, and fights over "Why is your ex texting you?" and makeup sex in the Caribbean. A tiny sliver of compressed coal, forged by the blood of mutilated African children, is bought at the price of a car, and is displayed on the woman's left hand so she can brag about it to her friends. "Look at how much I'm loved!" They nod and feign shouts of excitement, masking their insecurity over this reminder of their own romantic failings.

A year is spent in perpetual stress over momentous decisions about the type of font to be used on the wedding invitation and the color of the bridesmaids' dresses. When all is said and done, the wedding industry will have swindled tens of thousands of dollars out of the female's desire to indulge in a few hours of socially acceptable narcissism. The amount spent would have been enough to send their kids to college or more altruistically, could have been used to buy enough common medicines and immunization shots to save the lives of 250 African children. Later, the couple will fight incessantly over money.

Amidst all of this, generally around the 18-month mark of the relationship, a lull is experienced, coinciding with a reduction in the production of certain brain chemicals responsible for the passions and delusions over their partners above average adequacy. Behaviors that were previously seen as adorable now seem grating. She begins to henpeck every little action of his that doesn't mesh with her childhood fantasy of marrying Prince Charming. He stops pretending to care about her petty dramas and gossip. In public, his eyes wander to other women with the penetrating gaze of a predatory carnivore. She reaches out to an old flame on social media.

When given as a mere average, reports on the frequency of marital sex are bound to overestimate the number for those long past the bloom of their nuptials. I once queried a friend about his sex life now that he had just celebrated his tenth year of "incarceration" (his term, expressed with a feigned jocularity). He responded, "It was pretty good on the night of our anniversary, and I'll let you know in another six months when we do it again." The infrequency of sex among married couples is so common it may be appropriate to ask: Is this just human nature?

If it is, we would expect to see a similar pattern in the number of times HG's have sex. And there is indeed evidence of some decline in sexual activity in HG societies as couples age. Before the age of 30, Aka tribe members report having sex with their spouses 3.1 times per night. But the sexual activity of couples between the ages 30 of 45 sees a dramatic drop off, down to a mere 2.8 times a night!

Between the ages of 18 and 45, Aka couples average seven-to-eight acts of coitus per week, the usual pattern being to have sex three times a night, take a couple days off to recuperate, and then resume activities. What is the explanation for this insatiable female sexual appetite? They say everything in life has a silver lining. In this case, it's the upside of a lot of dead babies.

The precariousness of infant life in HG society spurs women to make full use of their fertile years. Although the goal of procreation takes precedence, sex is not without enjoyment. The Aka women orgasm at least once before sunrise.

A Hadza Love Story

Ostensibly, Oswo's excuse for heading over to the neighboring camp a dozen miles away was to discuss game patterns. That is what he told his friends, anyway, though the true reason was the swirling rumors that a young girl of that clan had blossomed into a beautiful 17-year-old woman. At 21, it was time to find a woman to live with, to clean his hut, fetch his water and comfort him at night.

He had spotted the young woman soon after entering the camp. Her smile, her eyes, those plump, perky breasts. He saw that her legs were fit and her rump curved from hours of unearthing tubers. Signs of fertility abounded.

Ishka had noticed him too, particularly the way he stole furtive glances at her when he thought she wasn't looking. Although she pretended not to be aware of his presence, she made sure to be seen as having fun and giggling with her friends whenever he was in the vicinity. Her friends whispered that he was a great hunter and had already killed three baboons.

A conversation began. A stroll through the bush, some innocent hand-holding, the removal of thorns from the other's shoulders, and then kisses.

He would not be returning to his camp.

What is meant by marriage in Hadza society? Is there a big ceremony, lifelong vows, till-death-do-us-part affirmations? No, marriage is a useful term anthropologists use to describe the living arrangements of hunter-gatherer couples. In truth, it simply means that a man and woman will start sleeping in the same hut. Oswo and Ishka will fall madly in love, and their constant lovemaking will result in a beautiful Hadza baby. But if you are expecting a fairy tale, a heartwarming saga of everlasting love and happiness, don't hold your breath.

While living with the Hadza, Michael Finkel noted that marriage in hunter-gatherer tribes was not devoid of bickering. "It's your turn to fetch the water," "Why was the meat not properly cooked?", "Why are you napping instead of hunting?" Women think men are lazy. Men think women nag. In short: The human condition.

Years later, Oswo will visit another nearby camp and flirt with a woman there. He'll make love to her. Back home, Ishka will hear of her husband's philandering through the grapevine. When he returns from his trip, he will find that he is no longer welcome in his hut. Not long after, she will take up residence with a new husband. Oswo will feel sad. He did not want his wife to leave him. He just wanted a little action on the side.

Think of the marriage advice we commonly hear. Phrases such as "A good marriage takes hard work." "A good marriage involves lots of sacrifice." Or, as Montaigne put it: "A good marriage would be between a blind wife and a deaf husband."

Lifelong and exclusive monogamy is not part of *homo sapiens* DNA. If it were, we wouldn't find marriage so difficult. We are best described as serial monogamists, who will, if the right opportunity arises, engage in discreet sex with other partners we find attractive. It's how we have done things for millions of years. A study of the Ache tribe of hunter-gatherers showed that the average woman would have had ten spouses by the age of 30, and had children with at least two of them.

How then to use this knowledge to improve relationships in the 21st century? If you're expecting me to offer some ingenious solution to this problem, I'm sorry to disappoint you. This is one of the cases where village life is so radically different from contemporary society that no easy fix presents itself. Many couples stay together in loveless marriages because they have erroneous views about the nature of human romance: It should last forever, and if it's not working we must be doing something wrong; we should stay together for the sake of the children; I can't stand giving away our fortune to divorce lawyers. None of these were problems for our ancestors. Without any tradition of lifelong marriage, people were expected to switch partners many times over the course of their lives. Since infidelity was so rampant, and everyone in the tribe at best distant relatives, a father could not be sure that the child was actually his. Consequently, paternal investment was very low among our ancestors. Children were nursed by their mothers until they had a certain degree of autonomy, and then were free to run around the village and do as they pleased. There was no need for lawyers and judges to arbitrate custody battles. No wars were fought over who got the house and the fine china collection. The hut they lived in would be knocked down in a month when these nomads moved camp, and the water bucket was easily replaced.

Perhaps we should use this knowledge to develop a more realistic approach to human relationships. We should not expect our significant others to love and desire a single partner throughout their lives. They will be attracted to other people, and temptation might get the best of them. Their desires don't mean that we are somehow unworthy; it just means that our partner is human.

The Piraha give us an example of an emotionally healthy response to infidelity. Dan Everett once walked into the hut of a couple to see the woman seated and the man lying in her lap. She was smacking him in the head as punishment for spending the night in another woman's arms. He was apologizing, and pretending to be more hurt from the smacks than he really was, while she cursed him out and pretended to be angrier than she really was. Their feigned screams of anger and pain were interrupted by bouts of giggling.

Psychedelics

I sat high up in a tree in the middle of campus. It was the last day of the school year at University. Co-eds passing underneath gazed up to notice three laughing freshmen resting 30 feet up on the oak tree's branches. After having exhausted voyeuristic thrills from the vantage of our lofty perch, we climbed down and headed to the campus garden where we chopped down a few bamboo trees. We slung the bamboo chutes over our shoulders and marched around the brightly colored roses and daffodils bathing in the afternoon sun. My two friends and I had ingested a bag of magic mushrooms.

Have you ever wanted to visit Never Neverland for a day? That's how I describe the wonders of a psychedelic trip to the uninitiated. Like the characters in Peter Pan, who remain day after day in an everlasting youth, the subjective experience of time under the influence of magic mushrooms crawls to a halt. What in reality is only hours seems an eternity. We may have been simply walking around campus, but to us we were on an epic journey, with every new tree, every open field, every garden a new adventure to be had. The beauty of the world overwhelming. Had I ever truly immersed myself in the wondrous efflorescence of a flower before? Was the dance of the clouds across the azure sky always this delightful?

My friends and I made endless jokes, laughing until our eyes teared up. We also had profound philosophical insights during our altered state of consciousness. Despite the occasional harmless bout of paranoia (we thought we were being stalked by a bald, female dwarf), we all agreed that up until this point, the day had been the best of our lives.

As the high began to wear off, I separated from my friends and headed back to my dorm room. On my computer screen was an instant message from Katie. With long legs, large breasts and a model's face, she was the best-looking girl in the freshman class. I'd had a crush on her for a year. Did she feel the same way about me? I intended to find out. I wasn't so experienced dealing with women back then, and had failed to make any serious headway, despite several invitations to her room late at night to "study." "Who wants to study at this hour?" I used to ask myself. This time, I had my head screwed on right. Or so I thought. Yes, I would come over to smoke a few bowls to celebrate the end of the school year.

I sat on the bed admiring her figure as I inhaled the potent marijuana smoke. I was nervous and excited about the possibility of sleeping with such an exquisite beauty. I gazed into in her emerald eyes. I felt my heart palpitate. A quick peek at her cleavage. Blood pumping to an obvious organ. Still high from the magic mushrooms, I told her about my adventures, as we smoked a second bowl. The marijuana seemed to be enhancing the effects of the shrooms. She was laughing and inching closer. This is it, I thought. The time is now. Then, just as I was about to make my move, I noticed something strange.

I was floating out of my body.

It was time to abort. I awkwardly excused myself and headed back to my dorm room. Now I'm sure someone watching me would have simply seen a freshman with a strange look on his face scurrying across the quad. But in my subjective experience, I was warping fifty feet at a time through campus until I got to my room. I lay down on my bed as I continued to float out and above my body for the next three hours. Meanwhile, the world kept going black and turning into a kaleidoscope whenever I closed my eyes.

Evidence that people ingested magic mushrooms dates back to 5000 B.C.E in Northern Algeria. Cultures in Central and South America left behind sculptures of Mushroom Gods, including Piltzintecuhtli, the God of the Divine Mushroom. Spanish explorers wrote of the use of these mushrooms by the Aztecs as early as 1502, when they were served at the coronation of Montezuma II. The Spanish conquerors quickly forbade the use of these potent plants, believing that the mushrooms allowed the natives to communicate with the devil. Their use continued in secret, however, in mountain villages beyond the reach of the invaders, in ceremonies passed on down through the generations.

R. Gordon Wasson, who was a vice president at J.P Morgan, visited one of these villages with his family and a few friends in 1955. They would become the first Caucasians in recorded history to participate in one of these ancient ceremonies. They were led by the shaman Maria Sabina. Wasson would write about his experience in *Life Magazine*, and a horde of westerners would descend upon this rural village, including the likes of John Lennon, Bob Dylan, and Mick Jagger. Like any other remote place in the world, once the tourists turned up, the indigenous culture and ritual suffered.

At the time Wasson ingested the mushrooms, no one knew what it was that made them such powerful conduits of psychedelic experience. Wasson brought the mushroom spores to Albert Hoffman, the inventor of LSD, who isolated the psychoactive chemical and found it to be psilocybin. Today, these mushrooms are cultivated in great quantities all around the world, and are in easy reach of your typical college freshman.

The profundity of a psychedelic trip is impossible to explain to one who has never tried such substances. Take a large enough dose and you are guaranteed to have the most intense experience of your life. It is not uncommon to feel a changed person afterward, sometimes for better, sometimes for worse, depending on the quality of your experience. It is not hyperbole to say that a trip can be so glorious you will think you are in a fairy tale; or, if things take a bad turn, one so harrowing you might as well be the character in Edward Munch's painting *The Scream*. These bad trips could largely be avoided if the hallucinogens are taken in the right circumstances, after the right preparation, and with a sage guide. The way Indians have been doing it for thousands of years. After all, as Maria Sabina once lamented, the mushrooms are meant to be medicine.

I learned a lot about myself from my mushroom trips, but I took away two very important insights that I could generalize about more widely. The first is the innate human need to go on a quest. A rite of passage for our ancestors, but nowadays something you mostly see in the movies. The emotional intensity, the adventure, the opportunity to delve into your mind and see what you find out about yourself. The insanely slow passage of time that makes those six hours seem like eons. This is why a psychedelic experience is aptly referred to as a "trip".

The second generalization regards the absolute beauty of the world that is right there in front of us at all times, but largely ignored. Dr. Richard Alpert, the Harvard psychologist turned psychedelic explorer, wrote a book in the sixties, coauthored with Sidney Cohen, the head of the federal drug commission. Alpert was to be the bad guy, espousing the positive view of psychedelics, Cohen deploring the negative effects. When they went to pick out photos for the book, the two authors couldn't agree on what a typical psychedelic drug user looked like. Cohen wanted pictures of people seeming to be wiped out, while Alpert wanted pictures of people skipping through flowers. There was only one photograph they both wanted. A picture of a guy lying on the floor looking at some spilled Coca-Cola. Cohen thought this was a good representation of how drugs waste our minds to the point where we do something so trivial and useless as staring at some soda. Alpert liked it because in that single drop of Coco-Cola abided the majesty of the universe.

My next illicit drug experience took place on Halloween, at a warehouse rave being DJ'ed by some of the finest electronic musicians on the planet. I had just ingested two pills of pure MDMA and the music seeped through my body and brought a euphoric smile to my face. Women, dressed as playboy bunnies and Marilyn Monroe, had never looked so sexy, so tempting. I felt like a shark in mating season. I approached them without the slightest self-doubt. On MDMA, the simple touch of another person's finger on your forearm feels amazing. The touch of their skin, their lips as we danced under the strobe lights was pure ecstasy. For many, this heightened sensual pleasure is all they will get from the experience. For me, it was much more profound. The waves of compassion that flooded my being would change me as a person. How silly all the neurotic tendencies and petty concerns of normal consciousness seemed in comparison to the confidence and loving-friendliness that poured out of me now. I was overcome by a sense that we are all in this together and that empathetic joy was the only reasonable response to living in a world with other people. This was the best I had ever felt, and the link between happiness and goodwill towards all was now ingrained in my brain. Well-being consists in loving and being connected with your fellow man -- and having orgies with your fellow women.

The following day, the bliss from the previous night was still there, but the next week I felt a bit more anxious, even a bit depressed. The drug had caused my brain to release unnatural amounts of serotonin, and I was now depleted of this precious neurotransmitter. I would not be right again until my brain had restored its natural balance. Subsequent ingestions, while still pleasant, would not produce the same magic as before. The down was no longer worth the high. And that's the problem with drugs. You *always* come down. I loved the feeling of ecstasy, but I would need to find a way to feel it naturally, without the side effects. Could this be done? Is it possible to recreate that overwhelming sense of empathetic joy, connectedness and self-confidence that one has on MDMA without burning out your serotonin receptors? Is it possible to capture the wonder of the universe without the risk of having a traumatically bad trip? Is it possible to view the world in a way where you are steeped in wonder, compassion, and beauty and yet still be functional at the same time?

In search of a way to retain the glow of his psychedelic experiences, Dr. Richard Alpert traveled to India. Here he fell under the spell of a guru and changed his name to Ram Dass. Through meditation, he learned that he could have these wonderful experiences of peace and unity naturally. By training the mind, one could replicate the focus, harmony and goodwill experienced on drugs, without ever having to come down or worry about overdosing. It was a skill first mastered by Paleolithic man.

IV. TRAINING THE MIND

Shamans

Chuonnasuan is known as the last shaman of the Oroqen people, a hunting tribe living in northern China near the border of Mongolia. As a young boy, Chuonnasuan would attend the healing rituals of the shamans in his village and try to mimic their behavior. His imitations were so convincing that his elders said he might one day grow up to be a master shaman himself. It was in his blood, after all. His grandfather was a Shaman, as well as his paternal uncle, a man of such great power that he was said to be able to kill a pig solely through the use of spirits.

But one cannot choose to be a shaman the way one chooses to be an accountant or a lawyer. The spirits must choose you. At the age of 16, Chuonnasuan's younger brother and sister died. The trauma caused Chuonnasuan to become withdrawn. He would go off into the forest alone to wander aimlessly in a trancelike state.

Fearing that Chuonnasuan might not survive the death of his siblings, his mother took him to a distant county to visit a powerful female shaman named Wuliyen. Her fee for performing a healing ritual of this magnitude was a horse, but Chuonnasuan's mother was too poor and didn't have a horse to give. Sensing the great potential within him, Wuliyen agreed to heal him anyway. The healing ritual lasted three nights, as Wuliyen danced around him, beating her drum, singing songs and sacrificing animals to the spirits. According to Chuonnasuan, one by one the spirits would enter his body, getting to know him and teaching him how to dance. As the spirits took control of him, he got up and followed Wuliyen around while she danced. He was at the whims of the spirits and unable to hear or speak for himself.

The three-day ritual cured him of his depression, and from that point on he would occasionally serve as a "second spirit" -- an essential assistant of a shaman. All went well until three years later he fell ill again. Although Chuonnasuan interpreted the cause of his sickness to be new spirits entering his body and fighting with the spirits Wuliyen had put in a few years before, the truth is that he had fallen ill after another traumatic tragedy. His young wife had died from illness, and Chuonnasuan yearned to be alone. For six months, he would sit under a tree while the spirits talked and sang to him from a distance. Finally his mother got involved again. She enlisted the help of his Uncle Minchisuan, a shaman, to perform the healing ritual. This time, a dance of only three nights was not sufficient. It took six full days of healing rituals and the sacrifice of many animals before Chuonnasuan was finally cured.

His uncle introduced him to the most powerful spirit of all, that of the two-headed eagle. With the spirit eagle by his side, Chuonnasuan's powers began to grow and he was asked to perform healing rituals of his own. He would continue to heal people for the next five years, curing one boy of his seizures and another woman of a skin infection, without the use of any medications.

Chuonnasuan's path to becoming a shaman follows the typical pattern outlined in Marcel Eliade's famous work *Shamanism: Archaic Techniques of Ecstasy*. The future shaman is usually the relative of past shamans, becomes mentally ill during his adolescent years, and is then healed and trained by an accredited shaman.

The word "shaman" comes from the ancient religions of northern Asia and was introduced to the West when Russian forces conquered these shamanistic people in the 16th century. Since then, scholars have used the term to describe the magico-religious practices of peoples all over the world. Shamans and closely related witch doctors and medicine men are found in traditional societies ranging from the Arctic to Africa to the Amazon. It is believed that these practices date back to the Paleolithic age. While shamanism differs in many important ways across these various societies, the key that ties them together is the ability to produce a trancelike state, and access to what they believe is the supernatural world of spirits.

A trance is an altered state of consciousness that is characterized by a focused attention, loss of awareness of the outside world and fuller access to the unconscious mind. A trance can range from typical daydreaming to one's body going completely limp, with all access to the outside environment completely cut off. Shamans have various techniques for inducing trances, including the use of hallucinogens, but they also employ non-chemical means such as dancing, singing and drumming. The San Bushmen of the Kalahari Desert are known for their trance dances. The women in the tribe sit around each other in a circle, clapping together and singing. The men circle around them, taking short, pounding, rhythmic steps with full concentration. This dance will go on for up to 10 hours and requires an inhuman amount of endurance, but with each step the Bushmen fall deeper and deeper into their trance state. In Siberia and the Arctic, shamans will use a drum that they beat rhythmically, first slowly and then picking up speed to four to seven beats per second. Some scientists believe that this rhythm increases the brain's theta waves, thereby helping to induce the trance.

Once in a trance, the shaman reports leaving this sphere of reality and enters the realm of benevolent and malevolent spirits. These spirits usually take the form of persons or animals with which the shaman communicates. If the spirits are evil, the shaman will call on friendly spirits to help drive them away. Or the shaman might evoke wise spirits to glean their wisdom in solving a problem afflicting the community.

According to Dr. Robert Sapolsky of Stanford University, shamans today would be classified as people who have schizotypal personality disorder, a mild version of schizophrenia. While schizophrenics are often so overwhelmed by their delusions that they are unable to function in society, a schizotypal person is usually seen as someone who is eccentric but can function well enough to hold down a job, though usually one solitary in nature. The schizotypal person is drawn to odd beliefs and magical thinking. This is the person who is really excited by new age ideas, and believes in telepathy, homeopathy or telekinesis. She will mistake ordinary life events as having an unusually profound meaning for her. Occasional quasi-psychotic episodes with intense illusions and auditory hallucinations can occur. Just as with the shaman, the onset of these psychotic episodes usually occurs after a stressful event during one's adolescence.

Schizotypal is a disease with a strong genetic basis. It is curious that a gene that is so detrimental to health and could lead to such a destructive form of schizophrenia would continue to propagate itself down through the generations. After all, bouts of psychosis are rarely listed as a virtue on most respected dating websites. But back in the day, having "magical abilities to commune with the supernatural realm through song and dance and cure your illness" was like being a rock star, a doctor and a cult leader all rolled into one. Hence the gene carried on, and schizotypal exists in about two percent of the population. This correlates perfectly with a tribe of 100 people having one active shaman and a shaman-to-be kinsman waiting in the wings.

Shamans profess to gain access to a hidden world of spirits during their trances, but we can dismiss their claims, knowing that their visions are a result of schizotypal hallucinations. The schizotypal person will experience hallucinations concordant with their society's spiritual paradigm. The shamans of the San Bushmen say that when they are in a trance they communicate with the spirits of their dead ancestors and these ancestors tell them where to find food and water in the desert they inhabit. The shamans of Mongolia talk to eagles and other animals, while the shamans of the Amazon communicate with the powerful spirit animals of their habitat such as the jaguar. In the middle ages, Christian monks who fell into a trance after a marathon prayer session had hallucinations of angels and demons. People born in the Midwestern United States in the latter part of the 20th century routinely reported being abducted by aliens.

All that said, the shamans have a lot to teach us about mental health. A group of scientists from the World Health Organization discovered something shocking: People diagnosed with schizophrenia fared better in developing nations than in advanced industrial societies. How could this be? Wouldn't access to first world doctors and medicine be more beneficial to them?

The answer can be found by examining how different cultures view the disease. A person in 21st century western society who claims to be a living god would quickly be locked up in the nearest asylum. But a schizotypal making those same claims in ancient Jerusalem might find his birthday being celebrated in distant lands thousands of years after his death.

While contemporary doctors consider periods of brief psychosis as an illness, this diagnosis gives their patients the impression that something is very wrong with them. The stigma associated with mental illness causes further problems, such as anxiety and depression. Stress is a major cause of psychotic symptoms in those who have a genetic predisposition to schizophrenia, and is a contributing factor in future breakdowns. It doesn't help that most schizophrenics have trouble keeping jobs. Hearing voices while you are trying to sell someone low-risk mutual funds is not the best way to make a sale. Financial instability and social ostracism only add stress, furthering psychotic symptoms. The schizotypal who became a shaman in prehistoric times was not only given a job, but the most respected job in the community. Considered to have special powers, shaman were looked upon as Paleolithic X-Men. This must have done wonders for their self-esteem.

In traditional societies, when a person succumbs to mental illness, the affliction is not attributed to something inherently wrong with the patient. The illness is due to evil spirits that have inhabited his or her body. These spirits will be driven away by a shaman during a healing ritual involving the whole community. Communal support, combined with the placebo and hypnotic effects of the trance, can help explain the healing prowess of the Shamans during these rituals. Those healed by the shaman may then go on and learn to become shamans themselves. While schizophrenics today continue to relapse into psychotic episodes again and again after being treated for their initial illness, according to Eliade, those in traditional societies are essentially cured once they have undergone shaman training themselves. Sure, they may have still have hallucinations (this is a genetic-based disease, after all), but these visions are now under the shaman's control. He or she can evoke these visions on command instead of being taken over by them unwillingly. How does shaman training accomplish this? The answer to this involves physical and mental training. The shaman, says Eliade, "displays a keen intelligence, a perfectly supple body and an energy that appears unbounded. His very preparation for future work leads the neophyte to strengthen his body and perfect his intellectual qualities."

In many cultures, the process of becoming a shaman required that the initiate pass through a series of ordeals. For the prospective shaman of the Shuswap tribe of British Columbia, the young man, after reaching puberty and before having ever touched a woman, would build a sweat-house at some distance from the village where he would go at the end of the day, spending the night dancing and singing songs, and only being allowed to return to the village in the morning. This process might go on for several years. The Manchu in China have a ritual where the prospective shaman must pass a test in order to show mastery over his body. In the dead of winter, nine holes are made on the ice surface of a frozen pond. The candidate has to dive into the first hole and come out through the second. Then he dives into that hole again and comes out through the third, and so on until he finally emerges for good out of the ninth hole.

To perform a healing ritual, the shaman must be able to dance, drum and chant for 10 hours straight. Try doing that three nights in a row, often while wearing an elaborate costume that weighs over 30 pounds. This takes an extraordinary amount of endurance and is the reason why the shaman undergoes rigorous physical training. Recent studies have concluded that exercise has a profound effect on the emotional well-being of schizophrenics, and often results in the reduction of symptoms.

The three-day healing ritual is not only physically taxing but mentally exhausting as well. To be able to chant continuously for such a long period of time takes a serious amount of focus. Take a break from reading and try clapping and saying "OM" on each clap and keep on going for as long as you can. How long before you get bored, think this is a stupid activity, or get distracted and quit? I bet you don't last longer than a couple of minutes; most of you will stop within 15 seconds. The shaman will begin his chanting and clapping while the sun is still up, watch the sun dip below the horizon, and when the sun comes back up again, the shaman will still be chanting away.

Both schizophrenics and schizotypals exhibit impaired attentional functioning. In fact, attention disorders are one of the best biological markers for future susceptibility to schizophrenia. Through his training, the shaman not only overcomes his attention impairment but develops a concentration power far above that of a normal member of his tribe. That normal member in turn has a concentration power orders of magnitude greater than the average person in our scatterbrained society. And as we will soon learn, a mastery over our ability to focus is the essential skill for developing extraordinary mental health.

As a result of his training, the shaman has evolved from a state of mental illness to a high degree of mental and physical functioning. The shaman also functions as historian and keeper of the tribe's esoteric knowledge. As part of his healing practice, he must be able to recall from memory the words to songs that he sings throughout the night. Attention and memory are the building blocks of a

191

high IQ. The end result is a person who is intelligent, energetic, and possesses great self-control. The anthropologist Karjalainen says that amongst the Yakut tribe the shaman "must be serious, possess tact, to be able to convince his neighbors; above all, he must not be presumptuous, proud, ill-tempered. One must feel an inner force in him that does not offend, yet is conscious of its power." Through shamanism, Paleolithic man chanced upon two great discoveries that will be the focus of the rest of this book: that of deliberate mental training and the role of the altered state of consciousness in producing ultimate well-being.

The Monks

From the beginning, Matthieu Ricard lived a charmed and stimulating life. Born in the idyllic French town of Aix-Les-Bains in the foothills of the Alps and surrounded by the beautiful Lake Bourget, he spent his winters speeding down the slopes, his summers sailing with his uncle, a daring navigator who was one of the first to travel solo around the world on a 30-foot sailboat. Aside from skiing and sailing, Matthieu's passions included wildlife photography and birding. He spent his weekends prowling through the woods searching for rare birds. At the age of twenty, he published a book on migratory animals. Intellectual queries came naturally to Ricard. His father was the renowned French philosopher Jean-Francois Revel, and his mother a lyrical, abstract expressionist painter. Matthieu's interests gravitated toward science, and he eventually earned a Ph.D. in molecular genetics, while working in the lab of a Nobel Prize winner at the Pasteur Institute. It seemed as if Matthieu had everything in life that he could possibly want. But at the age of twenty-six, he dropped it all, bought a one-way ticket to the Himalayas, and never looked back.

What prompted this dramatic change?

By any reasonable standard, Matthieu's life up until this point had been a resounding success. Yet he felt that something was missing. His parents frequented rarified intellectual and artistic circles, and he had met all the great writers, philosophers, painters and musicians of that era. Through his uncle, he met adventurers and explorers, all in all a very interesting bunch. In a 1960s French culture that revered intellectuals, these people were thought to have attained the very pinnacle of human existence, what everyone should aspire to. But while Matthieu admired the individual genius they displayed in their chosen endeavors, he realized that he had no desire to *become* like them. As Matthieu is fond of saying: "I would love to play chess like Bobby Fisher, but I wouldn't want to *be* Bobby Fisher." When it came to the qualities Matthieu considered the most desirable, such as altruism and *joie-de-vivre*, these high achievers were no better off than the average person.

Intrigued by a documentary depicting Tibetan monks who had fled the Chinese occupation, he traveled to Darjeeling, India, to meet these people who seemed to exude such serenity. Matthieu writes:

How to describe my first encounter with Kangyur Rinpoche, in June 1967, in a small wooden cottage a few miles from Darjeeling? He radiated inner goodness, sitting with his back to a window that looked out over a sea of clouds, through which the majestic Himalayas rose to an altitude of more than twenty-four thousand feet. Words are inadequate to describe the depth, serenity, and compassion that emanated from him.

That encounter would change Matthieu Ricard's life. From that moment on, it was only a matter of time before he would leave Paris for good and move to the Himalayas to train under the guidance of the meditation masters that he met there. For the next 35 years, Matthieu would remain in the Himalayas, living in a monastery, translating ancient works into western languages and acting as the French interpreter for the Dalai Lama.

In the late 1980s, an organization called the Mind and Life Institute began arranging dialogues between western scientists and the Dalai Lama. The original intent of these meetings was for the scientists to acquaint the inquisitive Dalai Lama with their latest findings, but the Dalai Lama surprised them with his perspicacious inquiries regarding the current state of neuroscience. Aware that meditation brought about radical changes in subjective experience, he wanted to know if meditation could actually alter the structure of the brain. Someone proposed that the scientists examine the brains of the monks, using the tools of modern science. Would the monks' claim that meditation made you happier be visible on a brain scan?

A neuroscientist by the name of Richard Davidson at the University of Wisconsin-Madison decided to observe the brains of some high-level monks chosen by none other than the Dalai Lama himself. Davidson selected Matthieu as his first test subject. By this point, Matthieu had lived in the Himalayas for over 30 years, including two-and-a-half years of solitary retreat. He knew that on the inside his meditation practice had done wonders for him. But could it be verified objectively?

Davidson placed hundreds of electrodes on the bald monk's scalp making him appear as if he were sporting white dreadlocks. Davidson asked Matthieu to do various forms of meditation while he recorded Matthieu's brain waves with an EEG machine. Matthieu also calmly meditated while in an fMRI, a place where many people refuse to go without tranquilizers. Later, Davidson compared Matthieu's results with a control group that had only been practicing meditation for a week.

Matthieu's results were off the charts. Literally. At first the scientists figured something must have been wrong with their equipment. If they had expected the monks to be happy, they hadn't expected the monks to be *this* happy. The machines were incapable of reading the amount of happiness generated by Matthieu. The machines would have to be re-calibrated and the experiment would have to be run again.

When accurate measurements were finally assessed, the researchers were amazed. Not only were Matthieu's results a complete outlier in regard to the control group, but they dwarfed anything ever reported in the scientific literature. Particularly of note was the gamma wave activity in the left prefrontal cortex. Previous research had shown that when people have high electrical activity in this area of the brain they report feeling happiness, enthusiasm, joy, energy and alertness. While meditating on compassion, the gamma wave activity in Matthieu's brain was 30 times higher than in the control group. But it wasn't just while meditating that Matthieu out-shined the control group. Matthieu's brain appeared more focused and happy even before he started meditating, providing evidence that meditation doesn't just make you happy while you meditate, but also carries over into the rest of your day.

Richard Davidson wasn't the only scientist interested in Matthieu. Paul Ekman, a world-renowned psychologist who studies the relationship between emotions and facial expressions, also wanted to study Matthieu. He designed four studies to gauge Matthieu's emotional intelligence. The first study tested Matthieu's ability to accurately read other people's emotions. Ekman had devised a video that shows the image of a person's face in a particular emotion such as contempt, anger, happiness or sadness. Matthieu would have to look at the face and tell Ekman what emotion they were experiencing. Was that contempt, or was that anger? Sound easy? Here's the rub, the images were flashed to Matthieu for as little as $1/30^{th}$ of a second. The images appear and disappear so quickly that your conscious mind doesn't have time to register it. Why do this? Because Ekman had found that people are really good at faking their emotions, but if you watch them closely you can catch that quick glimpse of anger before the person recognizes it in herself and forces a smile. People who do well on Ekman's test are excellent at understanding what someone is really feeling rather than how they portray themselves as feeling.

Of the more than 5,000 people that Ekman tested, Matthieu and another meditator, who had himself spent over three years in solitary retreat, turned in the two best scores ever recorded. While these results were astonishing, it was the second study Ekman performed on Matthieu that required him to rethink what he knew about human physiology.

Hardwired into the human brain is the startle reflex. Within a fraction of a second after hearing a loud and sudden noise like an explosion, the muscles around our eyes contract automatically. We have no control over it; even police officers that routinely shoot guns still show the startle response when they hear the sound of a pistol firing. The region of the brain in charge of the startle reflex is part of our reptilian brain stem and lies outside of conscious control. Or so Ekman thought.

What does the startle response have to do with mental well-being? Ekman had found that the magnitude of a person's startle response correlated with how often they felt negative emotions like sadness, anger and fear, but that there was no relationship to positive emotions. The goal of Buddhism is to decrease suffering, meaning that if Matthieu's startle response was less than that of a normal person it would provide further evidence that he experienced less negativity and that his meditation practice was working.

Matthieu was taken to a laboratory where he was hooked up to machines that would read his heart rate and blood pressure, and videotape his facial movements. He was told that in the next 10 seconds a sound would go off. When the inevitable bang occurred, as loud as a gunshot being fired next to his ear, Matthieu didn't flinch. Unlike every other human being who had ever been tested, Matthieu was able to suppress the startle response in his facial muscles. He did this by going into a state of meditation called "open presence," where instead of trying to actively suppress his body's reaction, he allowed the sound to happen within the vast space of his awareness, just as a bird crosses the sky but leaves no imprint on the sky itself. To this day, Ekman is still unsure how Matthieu was physically able to accomplish this.

Meanwhile, Dr. Richard Davidson had devised another test to measure a person's happiness by scanning their brains. When people are depressed, the amount of activity in their left prefrontal cortex is greatly diminished. And as previously mentioned, when people experience joy, enthusiasm and other feel-good emotions, the activity in the left prefrontal cortex spikes up. Conversely, activity in the right prefrontal cortex is associated with negative emotions like fear and anxiety. The balance in a person's brain between activity in the left prefrontal cortex and the right prefrontal cortex is one of the key ways neuroscientists measure how happy someone is. Hook someone up to a machine and figure out the ratio between left prefrontal cortex activity and right prefrontal cortex activity and you can get a good idea what kind of temperament they have. Davidson collected data on 175 "normal" individuals and measured their left prefrontal cortex to right prefrontal cortex ratio. He then brought in a monk who was the abbot of one of the major monasteries in India. He wanted to get a measurement of the monk's brain ratio, not while he was meditating, but in his baseline everyday state, to see how it would compare to the ordinary people he had measured. Once again, the results were off the charts. The monk had tipped the scales way over to the left, far higher than anyone else ever recorded.

On the surface, it appeared to be indisputable that Matthieu and the Tibetan abbot were a couple of jolly old fellows. But studying just two people doesn't prove much in the realm of science. Since testing Matthieu, Dr. Davidson has had more than a dozen monks come through his laboratory. All of them have shown a similar cognitive profile to Matthieu. Every one of these monks had spent at least 10,000 hours meditating, with the more advanced monks reaching 40,000 hours. There was also a correlation between the amount of hours the monks meditated and how "happy" their brains appeared to be, providing strong evidence that it was the monks' meditation training that was producing these unbelievable results.

Bhante G

In October of 2014 I went on a meditation retreat at the Bhavana Society in the mountains of West Virginia. During the retreat, which is otherwise a silent affair, you can sign up for small group interviews with the head monk Bhante Gunaratana Henepola, abbreviated to Bhante G, for obvious reasons. The purpose of these group interviews is to ask Bhante G questions, ostensibly related to our meditation practice. However, one woman, strawberry blonde and middle aged, had a different concern. The monastery is located in the forest, and each night after meditating in the main meditation hall we had to walk back to our kutis (small personal cabins) through the pitch-black night with nothing but our flashlights to guide the way. I got lost more than a few times myself amidst the trees, wondering where I was, before stumbling upon some poorly defined trail and eventually finding my way back to my kuti.

Woman: Last night I had this horrible nightmare where coyotes attacked me on my way to my Kuti and just ripped my face off! And then today while I was meditating I was trying to focus on my breath, but the images of getting attacked by coyotes in my dreams kept popping up and I couldn't focus. I just kept thinking about the coyotes, and now I'm scared when walking back to my Kuti. I'm constantly looking out for coyotes. What should I do about this?

Bhante G: Are you normally scared of these animals in the forest?

Woman: No, I'm not usually scared of animals or the dark, but for whatever the reason I am now.

Bhante G: Let me tell you a story. Not that long ago, I was taking my daily walk when on the path not more than 20 feet in front of me I saw a huge animal with a very long tail. It was a mountain lion. I did not feel any fear. I just watched it and the cat just looked at me and we stared at each other for a while. Finally the cat got bored and wandered off. I continued on my walk and then turned around and took the same path on the way home. I thought to myself, I hope I see that mountain lion again, what a beautiful animal! And sure enough, there was the lion again. We stared at each other for a few minutes once more and I just thought "What a splendid creature." I did not fear that I was going to die. The next day I walked the same path again, and this time I came across a deer carcass that was half eaten. I realized that the mountain lion did not attack me because he was already full from eating the deer.

Me: So you had no primal fear reaction? No subconscious flight-or-fight response that kicked in?

Bhante G: No, I was not worried; I don't know why. Mountain lions are dangerous. I just read recently about how a mountain lion attacked a boy and his mother who were hiking in the woods. The lion pounced on the boy first, so the mother started throwing sticks and stones at the lion. The lion then turned his attention towards the mother and killed her. Another time I was walking along and I saw two little bear cubs. I knew that the mother must be close by, and we all know that the most dangerous time to run into a bear is when it's a mother protecting her cubs. But I did not feel fear. I was curious to see the mother bear. What a beautiful creature she would be! So I just stood there until she showed up and just like when I saw the lion we just stared at each other until the bear walked away. Now before I go on my walks I always tell people where I am going, so that if one day I am attacked by a lion or a bear they will know where to find my body and they don't have to go searching all over for it.

That settled the issue in Bhante G's mind and he moved on to the next question. I looked over at the woman to see if Bhante's response had calmed her. What I saw on her face instead was: *Before I was ONLY worried about coyotes. I didn't even know if there were coyotes in these woods! Now you're telling me there are lions and bears!*

I later asked Bhante G about his own mental state, whether he had completely rid himself of suffering? "No, no, I am not fully enlightened. Yet!" he said with a smile. There was still work to do, even at age 87. "But I never worry, I never feel anger. Sometimes as my monks know, I get irritated, but it never leads to anger."

A man who never worries, not even when standing face to face with a lion. Not even when one of the engines of the commercial jet he was in burst into flames at 30,000 feet over the Pacific Ocean on the way from Hawaii to Sri Lanka. His reasoning? What would worrying accomplish at that moment? Would worrying make the fire go away? No. Better to enjoy those moments, which could well have been his last, and admire those spectacular colors produced by the flames.

Positivity Challenge

When I visited the Waorani, the closest any member of the tribe came to expressing a negative emotion was a look of contemplation on a man who was recovering from a poisonous snake bite. I asked the man if the Waorani ever get angry, and he said, "Never." I asked him if he ever felt stress. He had no idea what the word meant. I asked him if the Waorani ever worried about the future. He said he didn't know what would happen in the future, but today was good. The first mind-training activity I'm going to have you do is designed to rid your mind of the pervasive negativity that is endemic to the modern world. It will be the most life-changing week of your entire life. And it begins now.

For the next week, you are going to watch your mind like a hawk and observe the thoughts that surface. They will be positive, they will be negative, they will be neutral. You will have emotions, moods, and as soon as you notice any of them becoming negative you will squash them like a bug and reframe the situation as a positive one. You are walking out of your house, feet getting soaked by the slushy snow and your car is freezing. Good, it builds character. By putting up with the cold, you are learning to be tougher. The freezing cold is going to make you more alert. It will make you feel alive! You will use your willpower to keep

203

yourself in good spirits. Feeling tired, run down? Find the serenity in that. Every situation has a silver lining, and you are going to dwell on whatever that is.

Why do this?

The way you normally get into a bad mood is the following: A situation arises that you feel to be an impediment to some goal you are trying to attain. Let's say you have to go to the DMV in the morning. This involves skipping breakfast. You think to yourself: "I'm going to be starving, I don't even have time to stop at Starbucks for a latte!" This negative thought has activated a light stress response in your body. As your cortisol levels rise slightly, you are more likely to interpret the next few events as being stressful. You get outside, and the sun is hidden by a blanket of clouds. "Ugh, this weather. I need to move to California." More stress response. By now you are stressed enough that your attention span has diminished, and a song on the radio that you normally would enjoy isn't bringing the same lift. You switch back and forth endlessly between radio stations in a futile attempt to find something worth listening to. Then you get stuck behind a bus. "I'm going to get to the DMV late now, I'll be in line forever, and then I won't have time to do XYZ for the rest of the day!" By the time you find yourself surrounded by other bored-out-of-their-mind patrons at the DMV, your smartphone has lost its fascination, as you frantically switch back and forth between Instagram, Twitter and Facebook in search of anything to take your mind off the drudgery. "Hey, didn't I get here before that person? Why was his number called first? Look at his stupid face. I could just punch him."

These negative reactions to events are nothing more than bad habits. By breaking the negativity habit and replacing your old neuronal patterns with more positive ones, a situation that you once thought was a case of doom-

and-gloom simply doesn't have the same emotional connotation as before. We are going to begin The Positivity Challenge, or what Emmett Fox, the original mastermind of this endeavor, called the Seven-Day Mental Diet.

The Rules

You need to have one unbroken week of positivity in order to complete the challenge. That doesn't mean that negativity won't occur. Of course it will. The key here is that you can't dwell on your negativity. You can't let the negative thoughts that come into your mind proliferate. You have to let them go or transform them into positive ones immediately. If you catch yourself trapped in a negative train of thought lasting for more than one minute, you have to restart the challenge all over again on day one.

It would be an herculean feat indeed to complete all seven days without ever having to restart. Those that claim to do so usually aren't sufficiently aware of their thoughts to notice the subtle negativity that occurs. Or they might forget they are doing the challenge for hours at a time. What you need here is constant vigilance. You are likely to find that negativity comes at you like a rushing avalanche. "When will this meeting end?" You ask yourself. "Doesn't he understand how boring he is?" "Is that another gray hair? My head will be white by the end of the year!" All of these negative thoughts must be transformed into thoughts that are constructive. In addition to the growing positivity, your ability to watch your mind continuously will improve by leaps and bounds. Most of us are simply carried away by whatever thoughts and moods arise. This is a practice of distancing yourself from your own thoughts. You will learn more about your mind in this week than you will have in the previous decade.

It took me numerous attempts to complete the positivity challenge, most of the time I never made it through the first day. Hell, probably not even more than a few hours. Once I made it six-and-half-days before I succumbed to negativity. But I persisted. So should you.

After completing the challenge, you will notice a visceral difference in the way your body feels. You will be more relaxed, and habitual negative thought patterns will be replaced by more positive ones. When speaking to other people, you will notice how negative they are. You will hear someone say, "The world today, man, it's so awful." But instead of nodding in agreement you will ask: "Is the sun still shining?" "Is there a couple out there enjoying a great first date?" "Does music still make you want to dance?"

Tips

For the next week, the Positivity Challenge has to be the most important thing in your life. Your goal is a remarkable change in your habitual thought patterns. This isn't something to be taken lightly. It's not going to work if you only remember to do it from time to time. Go about your daily routine, but let the weight of these other concerns fade into the background. It's only seven days; your life won't go to shambles.

To be constantly aware of your thoughts, and to actively change them whenever they veer to the dark side, is strenuous. You are fighting against habits that have been ingrained in you for as many years as you have been alive. Do not underestimate the fortitude that is necessary. Emmett Fox said that fasting for seven days would be child's play compared to the difficulty of completing this challenge. He was exaggerating, but not by much.

It is not that you will suffer while doing the challenge. After all, you will be remaining in a state of positivity. It is that it takes extreme mental discipline not to fall off the wagon. I found it helpful to have constant reminders to be positive. I bought a bracelet that had the word "positive" written on it. As I walked down the street or drove in my car, I would repeat the word "positive" over and over, as if it was my mantra. The first few days are the most difficult, as the stream of negative thoughts will be at its most powerful. Once you have dammed the flow, you will find yourself beginning to automatically reinterpret potentially negative events as positive ones. The last few days will be easier. Or so you think. But by some cruel fate, just when you think you are settled in, some unexpected drama will try and kick you to the curb. Here is where you must stay true to your goal, or risk starting all over again.

If completing this challenge isn't something that interests you, you can go to a therapist, shell out thousands of dollars so that some complete stranger can analyze your thoughts, point out your negative and irrational beliefs, and change them into positive and rational ones. This is called cognitive behavioral therapy, and it is very effective in treating everything from anxiety ("What if this pain in my stomach means I have liver cancer?"), to depression ("I'll never amount to anything, what's the point of getting out of bed?"), to insomnia ("If I don't fall asleep right now, I'll be tired and miserable tomorrow!"), and even to procrastination ("I don't want to do work right now, I'm too tired, and it's boring; I'll do it later"). Or you can spend one week on the challenge I am proposing and make major headway on these problems -- and perhaps even eliminate them in one fell swoop.

Calm Concentration

Do you suffer from Obsessive Compulsive Delusion Disorder (OCDD)? Never heard of it? That's because OCDD is a term that is not found in the Diagnostic and Statistical Manual of Mental Disorders. If it were, nearly every single person on earth would suffer from it. The term was coined by B. Alan Wallace, a highly advanced meditator who worked as the Dalai Lama's interpreter before returning to California to get his Ph.D. at Stanford. Let's see if you meet the diagnostic criteria: Are you able to stay mentally quiet while still alert and awake when you wish to? That is, can you get your mind to stop talking, to stop thinking obsessively about any subject at any time and just remain in a calm quiescence at your voluntary control? Or is it the case that as soon as you wake up in the morning your mind is already blabbering to you? And stays blabbering to you all day long until you go to sleep? If so, then you may suffer from obsessive thoughts.

You have a compulsive relationship with your thoughts when you get caught up in your ruminations. You start thinking about a topic, say how your ex screwed you over and you are carried away down that river of thoughts like a class 5 rapid. You are not in control; your thoughts are in control of you. The delusional part comes in when you believe that your thoughts are an accurate portrayal of what is going on in the universe. As the saying goes: "I've known a lot of troubles in my life, most of which never happened."

Every one of us suffers from OCDD, and 99 percent of us never realize that we don't have to. Through mind training, we can cure ourselves of this ubiquitous malady. We can have the freedom to think about what we want to think about when we want to think about it, and to stay quiet and present when we don't.

B. Alan Wallace says, "If you were able to focus your attention at will, you could actually choose the universe you inhabit." What he means is that in any situation there are thousands of different things you could be focusing on, from the tactile feelings of your feet on the floor, the sounds going on around you, to the negative or positive thoughts regarding your boss's management style. The world as it appears to us is determined by what we focus on. And most people get caught up in whatever current of thoughts and sensations they happen to be experiencing without ever realizing they could be in direct control of their attention, like the commander of a ship. It is only when we have to do something boring like homework or taxes that we become aware of our inability to concentrate.

To remedy their lack of focus, people may drink a few cups of coffee or take stimulant medication. I've been there. After being diagnosed with ADHD I took those drugs for years. And they work remarkably well. But it's just a Band-Aid, and as soon as the drug wears off there are side effects. None of my doctors ever told me that the ability to pay attention could be improved through mental exercises.

The good news is that mind training offers not just a Band-Aid, but a potential cure for the wandering mind. Your attention span can be trained like a muscle, and the benefits of your newfound powers of concentration will be enormous. Being able to focus makes everything better and easier to learn. You can pick up new skills faster, your sex life will improve, and entering into a state of high concentration is in itself inherently pleasurable.

Psychologist Mihaly Csikszentmihalyi is the leader of research in what he calls "flow states." In a flow state a person is completely immersed in the activity that he is doing, channeling his emotions positively into the task at hand. There is a lack of reflective self-consciousness, as the person is totally absorbed and focused. If you have ever played a sport and been in the proverbial "zone," you know what this is like. If you have ever played an instrument or painted a picture and been so caught up in the moment that you have lost a sense of anything existing other than your performance, then you know what this is like. There is no boredom, anxiety or depression in a flow state. Instead, a flow state is marked by a feeling of joy or even rapture in the activity.

My time with the Amazonian tribes taught me that this kind of mindfulness was an evolutionary adaptation. Once while trekking through the jungle I was lost in my own thoughts, when a tribe member told me to watch my step and pointed to the ground. "Snake. Very, very danger. Poison. Like cobra," he said. I had nearly stepped on it. But my native companions were always in the here-and-now, listening to every little jungle sound, or in this case, on the lookout for any little sliver. To be mindful in the Amazon jungle is literally a matter of life and death.

Famed meditation teacher Shinzen Young had a similar experience meeting Amazonian and American Indians who have kept their culture intact.

"These Indians have the same eyes as advanced meditators," he writes. "Their lifestyle puts them into a meditative state." Unfortunately, ours does not.

If we want to be happy and calm, we need to return to the natural flow state of our hunter-gatherer ancestors. We can try to mimic their lifestyle as best we can, but we'll never completely get there. We need additional tools. Our ancestors would spend nights sitting by the fire, relaxing and watching the flames flicker. This was the first proto-meditation. Then they developed rhythmic dances and songs that took their baseline state of flow into deep states of ecstasy. You could do that too, but your roommates might think it's a bit weird that you spend your free time hopping around in a circle and wearing a feathered headdress. So I recommend meditation. With a consistent daily meditation practice of 30 minutes to an hour a day, changes in your baseline state of focus will be noticeable in a matter of weeks. Even more rigorous practice will prove exponentially more beneficial. A week-long retreat, fully absorbed in meditation from morning to night can be a life-changing event.

How To Meditate

Drukpa Kunley is known as the divine madman of Bhutan. A famous poet and master of meditation from the 15th century, he used shock methods to awaken the clergy out of their prudish and restrictive behavior. Upon meeting the legendary Tibetan monk Tsongkhapa, he was given a scarf as a ceremonial blessing. Drukpa proceeded to tie the scarf around his penis and wave it about in a rotating fashion.

A precocious child, Drukpa joined a monastery as a young man and spent a few years there before disrobing to wander the country as a mendicant. Walking into a new town, he would say things like: "Listen to me, all you people. I am Drukpa Kunley of Ralung, and I have come here today, without prejudice, to help you all. Where can I find the best booze and the most beautiful women? Tell me!" He would then visit the local watering hole, get drunk, tell stories, sing songs and deflower a few virgins. All ostensibly for the sake of their enlightenment. His penis is still known today in Bhutan as the "Thunderbolt of Flaming Wisdom."

Drukpa Kunley - Poem about happiness

I am happy that I am a free Yogi.
So I grow more and more into my inner happiness.
I can have sex with many women,

because I help them to go the path of enlightenment.
Outwardly I'm a fool
and inwardly I live with a clear spiritual system.
Outwardly, I enjoy wine, women, and song.
And inwardly I work for the benefit of all beings.
Outwardly, I live for my pleasure
and inwardly I do everything in the right moment.
Outwardly I am a ragged beggar
and inwardly a blissful Buddha.

He also wrote, "I practice the path of self-discipline. I meditate every day." And so must you.

Setting Up a Practice

It is best to set up a formal meditation practice that becomes part of your daily routine. A meditation session in the morning will give you a great start to the day. Make sure you are awake, though, do a few stretches, get some sunlight, take a shower or just splash your face with cold water. You don't want to still be drowsy while you meditate. Another session in the evening will help you relax and wind down. For busy people, I recommend that each of these sessions be 30 minutes long, or an hour of total meditation a day. Set a timer that will peacefully alert you when your time is up. Constant glances at the clock will interrupt your stream of mindfulness.

Skeptic: Are you nuts? I don't have an hour a day. When will I watch my television shows and read fake news articles? I can't possibly cut down on the nine hours a day I spend looking at a phone, computer or television screen!

A: Meditation won't take up an hour a day. It will make you more fully present for the other 23. And because you won't be distracted during every other waking hour, you'll find that you will be able to get everything you need to get done more quickly, more efficiently, and in the end you'll end up with more free time. But I guess if someone has a gun to your head, and that's really the only legitimate excuse not to meditate for at least 30 minutes a day, then do whatever you can. Whether it's five minutes or 10.

Now, there is a caveat for beginners. When you first start, you might find it difficult to meditate for 30 minutes straight. Your mind is just too crazy, and your body aches too much from the posture you are holding. In that case, start with 10 minutes per sit, and increase it by a few minutes each day until you reach 30. If you have time, sit for even longer. After a year, it shouldn't be a problem to sit for an hour straight. If you can meditate three, four or even ten hours a day, don't hold back! The rule for how often you should meditate is this -- As much as possible. Schedule these meditation sessions in your daily planner and stick to it. Eventually, it will become a pleasant habit to look forward to. No one's ever said, "You know what, I wasted too much time meditating."

Pick a place to meditate that is free of distractions. You should not be bothered by the chatter of conversation or other loud noises. You want it to be as quiet as possible. For those that live in the city and are assaulted by a constant stream of honking horns and police sirens, a pair of ear plugs is essential. If you like to meditate with your eyes open, then the space in front of you should be clear of any visuals that will catch your eye. A blank wall is fantastic.

Posture

You don't have to assume the full lotus position to meditate. In fact, there are only two rules that you should keep in mind when finding a posture for meditation:

1) Keep your spine straight, all the way up through your neck. There is a physiological reason for this. With a straight spine, you are more attentive. With slumped shoulders, your body falls into a stupor. Your eyes can be closed or slightly open, your gaze directed either straight in front of you or slightly downward.

2) Assume a position that will be comfortable for you to remain still in for the duration of your meditation session. You don't want body parts to start hurting or going numb. Nor should you be shuffling around all the time. You want to keep your full attention on the breath. If you want to sit in a chair, you can sit in a chair. That is perfectly fine. Personally, I like to place a zafu cushion on top of a yoga mat and sit on the edge of the cushion. Both my knees will touch the ground with one leg resting in front of the other. This is called Burmese style. If you can lie flat on your back without getting sleepy, that position is also acceptable.

Westerners have trouble with any sitting position that involves keeping the back straight. We are so used to being slouches that our hip and back muscles will ache after only a few minutes. Well, tough it out. After a week you will be able to hold your spine straight without any problem. People will comment on how your posture has improved. If you are sitting on a cushion, a common complaint is pain in the knees. Again the advice here is to tough it out for a while. If you can sit Burmese style at first for only five minutes before the pain becomes too distracting that's fine. The next time you meditate try and hold it for seven minutes. Eventually, you will be able to work your way up to an hour or even more. When I first saw Bhante G in the meditation hall, it was so early in the morning that the sun had yet to rise. I could only see his outline through the dim candlelight. He was meditating and sat so still and erect that it took me a while to realize that he wasn't a statue!

Mindfulness of Breathing Meditation

Take a minute to settle into your posture. Get yourself comfortable, but keep your spine upright. Meditation involves a balancing act between vigilance and relaxation. Too much vigilance and we will become tense, strained and wear ourselves out. Too relaxed and our minds will become dull or even fall to sleep. Become aware of the sensations of your body and notice what is going on there. Slowly bring your attention to the sensations of the breath going in and out of your body. Meditators debate as to just where in the body we should focus on the breath. Some say at the tip of the nose, some say at the abdomen, others just the entire feeling of the breath. I don't think it matters; just do what comes naturally to you.

As your breath goes in and out, keep your focus on the sensations caused by the breath cycle. Just feel the movement of the breath. Note when it reaches the apex of the inhalation, the short time when your breath is full and that brief pause after exhalation when you no longer have any air in your lungs. Keep your mind on the breath throughout the entire duration of its cycle. If you notice you are having problems becoming too tense or to dull, then balance yourself out by arousing your awareness on the in-breath, and then relaxing deeply on the out-breath.

Don't pull your breath. This is trickier than it seems. Don't force yourself to breathe slowly, or more deeply so that the physical sensations become more palpable. Just let your breath be. Just watch it. However you are breathing is fine.

Inevitably, your mind will wander from the breath. As a beginner, this will happen quickly. You will start thinking about your day, things you still have planned to do, a conversation you just had with someone, or thoughts about your meditation: "Am I doing it right?" "I think I'm doing ok." "Just focus on the breath." Whenever you catch yourself caught up in distracting thoughts, just gently return to the breath. Don't be frustrated that you were thinking. That will make it worse. Just relax and go back to the inhalations and exhalations of your breath.

If you are having difficulty concentrating, then experiment with counting the breaths. Watch the breath come in fully, noting the quick pause before the exhalation beings. After the air flows out and you reach the end of the exhalation, silently note "one." After another cycle of inhalation and exhalation, note "two." Keep counting all the way up to ten and then start the counting over again at one. If at any point you have forgotten what number you are on, just start over at one. Once you feel that your concentration has become strong again, stop counting and return to just the feeling of the breath.

Progress

A common analogy is to describe the beginner's mind as that of a waterfall. As you try to focus on your breath, you are distracted by a flood of thoughts, images, sensations, sounds -- and who knows what else. This is "the monkey mind." You will not be able to focus on your breath for more than a few moments before getting lost in some daydream. Minutes will pass before you realize, oh yeah, I was supposed to be meditating! This is normal. If you could focus completely on your breath without distraction from the very beginning, there would be no need to do this type of meditation. The more you practice, the longer you will be able to sustain your focus on the breath, and the less you will be bothered by distractions.

Think of it as a seesaw. On one end are all the things that distract you from the breath, such as thoughts, images, sensations, etc. On the other side of the seesaw is your attention to the breath. When you are just starting out, all the distractions will dominate and you will have only intermittent attention to your breath. You will watch your breath for a few counts of ten, and then get lost. Eventually, you will be able to stay with the breath longer and longer. The times when you are completely lost in a daydream will diminish. The distractions will still be there in the background, but they won't be strong enough to completely pull you away from the breath. At this point, the seesaw is about level.

The goal now is to increase the vividness and exclusivity of your attention to the breath. By "vividness," I mean the degree to which you fully perceive the breath. Noticing each moment of the breath as it comes in, pauses, and then goes out, not wavering from the breath at all during its duration. Exclusivity means that the background distractions become more and more subtle, and eventually disappear altogether for periods of time. There are now moments when you are singularly focused on the breath without any other sensations interfering.

Mastery of this type of meditation comes when you can maintain single-focused attention on the breath effortlessly, without distraction, and consistently when you meditate. When this happens, great joy, bliss, and tranquility will arise. Outside of your meditation sessions you will feel light, relaxed, and have exceptional mental balance.

<u>Metta</u>

"A human being is a part of the whole, called by us 'Universe,' a part limited in time and space. He experiences himself, his thoughts and feelings as something separated from the rest, a kind of optical delusion of his consciousness. This delusion is a kind of prison for us, restricting us to our personal desires and to affection for a few persons nearest to us. Our task must be to free ourselves from this prison by widening our circle of compassion to embrace all living creatures and the whole of nature in its beauty. Nobody is able to achieve this completely, but the striving for such achievement is in itself a part of the liberation and a foundation for inner security." - Albert Einstein

While loving our family comes naturally, and developing love for our friends is relatively easy, our feelings towards strangers we have never met are hardly ones of love. Might we feel curiosity about them? Sure. Might we extend overtures of friendship? Possibly. But do we feel a deep, profound love and compassion towards them? If you are like most people, the answer is no. Depending on the situation, there might be a bit of wariness regarding the stranger's intentions. Evolution has superb reasons for wiring us this way.

The majority of South American and Central American natives did not die from the swords and bullets of the

Spanish invaders, but from the smallpox they carried. Foreigners grow up in different environments, and are exposed to different viruses and bacteria to which people never exposed to these germs have no immunity. If you came across a stranger in ancient times, that person might be carrying a disease that could wipe our your whole tribe. Or they might want to seize our women or our land. In ancient times, it was better to have a healthy skepticism towards strangers until you were reasonably sure that they meant you no harm. But today's world is different. In first world countries, you can feel safe walking down most streets and do not have to worry that someone is going to harm you. The safety of the modern world makes it possible to spread our net of compassion to include not just close family and friends, but the entire world, just as Einstein advised.

Everybody Wants to be Happy

Engage in an exercise with me. I want you to vividly imagine someone you love. It could be a family member, a spouse, whomever, as long as you love them. Picture their face, or if they happen to be in the room with you right now, take a good look at them. As you are visualizing or looking at their face, use your capacity for empathy to imagine what it is like to be them. They are probably thinking about things they want to happen to them, things they hope to avoid. They are self-conscious about how others perceive them. They want to make a good impression. They want to be successful. They want things to go well for them. They want to be happy. In this regard, they are just like you.

If you found it easy to empathize with a loved one, now picture someone you don't know very well, someone you may have passed on the street. It could be someone sitting next to you on the plane, it doesn't matter who, just as long as you can visualize their face and your feelings are rather neutral towards them. Use empathy to imagine what it is like to be them. They too are thinking of things they want to happen to them, things they hope to avoid. They want people to like them, they want to be successful, they want to be happy.

Nobody wakes up and says, "I hope I contract syphilis today." People want to enjoy life, people want to be happy. But they are confused as to how to go about it. It is hard to remember that everyone you meet is struggling with hopes, dreams, desires for love and affection, just as you are. We need to remind ourselves that everyone wants to be happy, everyone wants things to go well for them, and everyone wants to avoid suffering.

Metta Meditation

Metta is a Pali word that is often translated to mean "loving-friendliness" or "benevolent goodwill." In metta meditation we first cultivate this feeling of metta towards ourselves, then our family members, and then gradually outwards until this feeling of metta encompasses the entire universe. Begin your practice by doing some mindfulness of breathing. When you feel that you have settled in, and your mind has calmed down, silently repeat the following phrase:

May I be well, happy, and peaceful
May I be well, happy, and peaceful
May I be well, happy, and peaceful

Keep on repeating this phrase, slowly and meaningfully. As you do so, visualize yourself being well, happy, and peaceful. Feel this happiness in your body. Try to enhance that feeling. The more you do it, the easier it will be to generate this feeling on command. Sometimes you won't be able to, sometimes, despite repeating the phrases over and over the feeling of loving-friendliness won't arise. That's ok. The more concentrated and calm your mind is, the easier it will become. The more you practice, the better you will get.

Repeat *May I be well, happy, and peaceful* for at least five minutes. Then move on to the following phrases. The instructions are the same as before, visualizing as best you can the other people being well, happy, and peaceful. Really try and feel their happiness. Repeat each phrase for five minutes and then move on to the next phrase.

May my family be well, happy, and peaceful
May my friends be well, happy, and peaceful
May all indifferent persons be well, happy, and peaceful
May all unfriendly persons be well, happy, and peaceful
May all beings be well, happy, and peaceful

A more advanced version of metta meditation involves imagining a glowing white orb of light at the center of your chest. The instructions begin the same as before; start your meditation as you normally would, with mindfulness of breathing. Once your mind has calmed down and you feel able to concentrate, begin to visualize an orb of white light in the very center of the chest. This light represents benevolent goodwill. With each in-breath, imagine the white light growing and expanding. Do this for a few minutes. When you can clearly visualize this orb, then on each out-breath imagine rays of this radiant white light infusing your entire body. As you do this, generate the feeling that this white light is filling you with loving-friendliness. On every out-breath visualize the rays of light leaving the orb in the center of your chest and infusing your head and limbs all the way down to your fingertips.

Once you have fully infused your body with benevolent goodwill, both in the visualization of white light throughout your body and in the positive feeling of loving-friendliness, then begin to imagine a loved one. Take the benevolent goodwill from that orb of white light at your chest and send those rays outwards until they hit the chest of the loved one you are thinking about. Continue for a few minutes, sending that ray of light into the loved one until their entire body is infused and you feel an abundant goodwill towards that person.

Now expand the direction of the white light by sending it out to everyone in the near vicinity. Repeat the previous steps as you imagine the blanket of white light shooting out from the center of your chest in all directions and infusing the bodies of everyone in your community. Do this for a few minutes and then expand the rays of light from your chest even further outwards. Imagine this bright white light covering the entire earth and all beings. Vividly imagine people on every continent becoming infused with this light. At this point, you should feel benevolent goodwill towards the whole earth. Stay here for a few minutes before continuing with one final step. Take the white light that is now covering the entire planet and expand it outwards until it flows through every nook and cranny of the universe. Your benevolent goodwill now engulfs the universe at large. If your concentration is strong, and you have completed this meditation with focus, you should now viscerally feel this loving-friendliness for the universe in your body.

Benefits of Metta

Metta meditation may seem similar to prayer, but it is not. Prayer involves the belief that your thoughts are going to reach some transcendent being who will answer them and make your wishes come true. In metta meditation one may wish for others to be happy, but there is no force that will make them come true. What will happen is that the act of saying these phrases will bring about changes in your own mind.

Numerous studies have catalogued the benefits of practicing metta meditation. They include an increased sense of well-being, with greater experiences of positive emotions and life satisfaction. Metta meditation makes people more likely to be helpful, increases their empathy and compassion, and decreases their bias towards other. It makes them more likely to increase their number of social connections. It reduces stress, mental illness and even signs of aging.

These studies show that the benefits of metta improve over time, as people get better at the meditation. And while these studies generally had participants meditating only about 15 minutes per day, metta has the advantage of being easily practiced far more often than that. You can practice metta not only on the cushion but as you go about your daily life. When you are cooking breakfast, repeat the phrases: May I be well and happy. May my family be well and happy. When you are walking down the street, wish that every person you pass be well and happy.

Metta also helps with concentration. If you are doing mindfulness of breathing and can't seem to focus on your breath, it can be helpful to switch over to metta practice until your mind calms down. Metta relaxes you, which pacifies the monkey mind, and the very act of repeating the phrases is an act of concentration in itself. When you mix metta with very strong concentration, the results become quite profound, and with a little practice one can radiate a sense of loving-friendliness for all the world. Einstein told us that we need to expand our compassion towards all of nature and its beauty. With metta meditation, we have a method by which we can turn this thought into reality.

Jhana - The Natural Ecstasy

What is your idea of ultimate pleasure? Perhaps it is being bathed in candlelight, the taste of perfectly aged wine on your lips, while being massaged with fragrant oils and worked into a fit of passion in preparation for making love to the girl of your dreams: your partner's better-looking best friend. Perhaps you think it takes more chemical assistance, like the rush of heroin coursing through your veins? Or maybe it's the standard line everybody falls back on: the moment of your child's birth.

What if I were to tell you that a pleasure exists out there that is more enjoyable than any of these things, without the side effects of jealous partners, overdosing or having to change diapers? That this pleasure is completely free, could be had at any moment in which you are able to simply sit quietly, and has no negative side effects? You probably wouldn't believe me, but it's true, my friends. It's true!

On my first long meditation retreat I settled into some good concentration by the fourth day. Using a combination of metta and mindfulness of breathing, my focus was stronger than it had ever been before. Distractions such as the sounds of people shuffling next to me ceased and my mind remained focused exclusively on the sensations of my breath. Joy began to creep up, and I decided to enhance it with some metta: "May all beings be well and happy." With my strong concentration, the metta had a cumulative effect and increased the joy I felt in my body. I continued: "May all beings be well and happy. May all beings be well and happy." The joy became even stronger and was palpable. I then switched from mindfulness of breathing to focusing directly on the joy. When I did this, the joy spread throughout my body, infusing my torso and limbs with a powerful, pleasant energy. When I tried to continue my metta practice, something odd happened. Although my eyes were closed, everything seemed to get brighter in this golden light. Also, I no longer felt as if I was intentionally uttering the metta mantra; instead the words and joy had control over me. The well-wishing for others' happiness had taken on a life on its own, and I was just along for the ride. I was completely immersed in this feeling of joy as it grew in intensity. The volume of the pleasantness and compassion for others became overwhelming, as if I might geek out right there in the meditation hall!

After the meditation session was over, we all headed into the tearoom to relax. As I sat down, I noticed a girl sitting across from me. She was looking at me and laughing. I had such a blissful aura I must have seemed totally high. Since it was a silent retreat and no talking allowed, I wrote a note to a friend who was on the retreat with me and passed it to her. It read: "I feel as if someone slipped me a molly." The bliss and joy would tone down a bit, but some form of it would remain with me for the last few days of the retreat.

What had just happened to me? I had simply sat down on a cushion, totally sober, watching my breath and wishing happiness for all and had entered a state of pleasure more intense than sex or drugs and without any of the adverse side effects. This was incredible! Was this the state of meditation known as jhana I had heard so much about?

Getting To Jhana

To achieve jhana, one's concentration skills have to be very powerful. It generally takes many months of serious practice of at least one to two hours per day as a good base, followed by an intense retreat, to make it possible. However, there are no rules stipulating how fast one can make progress in meditation, and the variety here is enormous! Once you have attained this level of concentration, further practice will help you to maintain it, and the bliss of jhana can be accessed at will. As meditation teacher Daniel Ingram puts it, when you have such strong concentration, you can either go home from work and crack open a beer, or sit on your meditation cushion and bathe yourself in as much bliss as you can possibly handle.

The first step is getting to access concentration, which I will describe in a little more detail now. With increased practice of mindfulness of breathing, you will become more focused on the breath, and distractions will fall by the wayside. As you do this, you will reach a point that the Buddhist monk Ajahn Brahm calls "the beautiful breath." Following the breath becomes delightful, and the discontent that is the source of mind-wandering evaporates. Distractions such as sounds, sensations, even thoughts will hardly register in conscious experience, if at all. You are fully and exclusively with the breath. This is access concentration. When you can remain here for 10 to 15 minutes, you are ready to go for jhana.

Switch your object of meditation from the sensations of the breath to a feeling of joy that should now be palpable within your body. Focus on the pleasurable feeling, and as you focus on it, that pleasurable feeling should intensify. At first, your mind might want to go back to the breath, or you might focus on the pleasure and it won't expand. If that happens, just rest back in access concentration for a moment and then try again. When you are able to maintain focus on the pleasurable sensations, and notice their expansion throughout your body, you are getting close to jhana. This may not happen in a linear way. The pleasurable sensations may grow a bit, stop, grow a bit more, etc. The key here is not to try and force it. You cannot will jhana to happen, it is not something that you do, but something that happens to you. All you can do is focus on the pleasure and let it happen. Eventually, the pleasure will expand to the point where it takes up your entire conscious experience. You will feel as if you have sunk into and completely immersed in this pleasure. It is obviously an altered state of consciousness. There is rapture, ecstasy, supreme delight. This is the 1st jhana.

But we can get even happier. Once you have mastered the first jhana, which can take days, or weeks or even longer, and can hold onto it for at least 15 minutes, then you are ready to move on to the 2nd jhana. The 1st jhana isn't completely satisfying due to that geeking-out quality I mentioned on my meditation retreat. There is a certain unstable feeling to the 1st jhana. In the 2nd jhana our attention moves away from these physical sensations of pleasure and focuses more on mental happiness and joy. The mind becomes intensely focused on these positive emotional qualities, and the instability of the 1st jhana is gone. The rapturous delight of physical sensations is still there, however, and eventually, believe it or not, these get tiresome. When this happens, you are ready to move on to the 3rd jhana.

The 3rd jhana is a much more serene state than the previous two. It is a state of deep, happy contentment that occurs when we let go of the energetic sensations that abound in the first two jhanas. Here one notices the difference between contentment and joy. Joy is that jumping-up-and-down quality, while contentment is more like an "'aaahhhh." The third jhana is the latter, only far more still, and far more powerful than anything you have experienced in normal life.

Amazingly, there comes a point where all feelings of happiness, bliss and even contentment get old. In the 3rd jhana there is a strong sense of stillness. In the 4th jhana this stillness turns into equanimity -- a state of astonishing imperturbability and peace. No happiness, no suffering, just a deep peacefulness that is all-pervading. There are more jhanas to go, but they are not about happiness but about entering the "formless realms". States of mind completely off the map from anything you could experience in normal reality. It is best at this point to get a meditation teacher to guide you through them.

The Science of the Jhanas

Scientists have studied the jhanas under experimental conditions. Wanting to know why meditators reported such extreme joy while in the jhanas, they hooked up a meditation master and had him cycle through the jhanas. They found that in the first few jhanas, the meditator activated the dopamine/opioid reward system in the brain. And although these experiences were subjectively reported by the meditator as being more joyful than multiple orgasms, the scientists did not find that the amount of activation in the dopamine/opioid system to be extreme. Instead, they explained that the subjective experience of such joy was in the signal-to-noise ratio.

In jhanic meditation, the meditator reports having his internal dialogue turned down. The mind becomes quiet. Scientists tested this by looking at the Broca and

Wernicke's area of the brain. These two parts of the brain are associated with language, and they were found to be significantly less active during jhana. Meditators also report less awareness of the external world, so the scientists sought to see if areas of the brain that process auditory and visual stimuli were less active. Once again, the scientists found this to be true. Because the meditator in jhana is less aware of external stimuli, as well as having his internal dialogue pacified, the pleasurable feeling produced by activation of the dopamine/opioid system becomes the sole focus of attention. Without anything internal or external to distract the meditator away from the pleasurable feeling, that feeling appears more intense than drugs or sex.

Extreme activation of the dopamine/opioid system has its downside, what every drug user calls a crash. This is due to a depletion of the neurotransmitters that caused the feeling of happiness in the first place. The brain has used them all up and now is deficient. Because the dopamine/opioid system in jhanic meditation is only moderately active in comparison to drugs, there is no reported crash, although the joyful feeling does vanish when the meditator cycles to the higher jhanas. Could this be due to mild dopamine depletion from the pleasurable lower jhanas? The scientists did find that activation of the dopamine/opioid system was less than in a resting state during the 5th jhana.

The meditator has another advantage besides not crashing over the drug user. Tolerance. The drug user will quickly build up tolerance to his drug of choice, and ever greater amounts of the drug will be needed to reach the level of that initial high. Eventually, as in addiction, the drug may not produce any pleasure at all. But the addict will still crave it. The jhanic meditator does not build up a tolerance to jhana; in fact, getting into jhana becomes progressively deeper and easier to do with practice.

What is Real Jhana?

Most of the people reading this book won't know about the great jhana controversy in the Buddhist community. But if you delve more deeply into books on jhana, or go on jhana retreats, you may hear different ideas of what constitutes real jhana, and what is just a facsimile. For those interested in investigating the jhanas further, and I hope all of you feel this way, it's worth mentioning a bit about the controversy here.

The confusion originates in the ancient literature, which gives varying descriptions of jhana. In the original *suttas* -- the speeches said to be given by the Buddha -- jhana is more easily attainable. In the later commentaries of the *suttas,* written by monks hundreds of years later, jhana has become something far grander. Jhanas are described as states that can only be reached by the most serious meditators, usually monks on very long retreats, and involves such fantastic feats as being able to sit in jhana for 24 hours straight. They are entered not from focusing on a pleasurable sensation, but what is called a *nimitta,* a spark of light that develops while you are in access concentration. In these jhanas the five physical senses and thought completely drop away. Someone could yell in your ear, even pick you up and drop you back down and you would be so absorbed in your jhana that you would never know it.

While the jhanas of the commentaries are far deeper, more profound, and even more blissful, the *sutta* jhanas that I have explained in this chapter are extremely nice in their own right. So much so, that a sexual embrace, a nose full of cocaine, and watching your child's first steps seem like suffering by comparison.

V. THE NATURE OF REALITY

This is a nirvana maze. Start in the center. Can you find
your way out of the maze to Nirvana?

The End of Stress

If you've read this far into the book and applied the tips to your life, you are probably a pretty chill person by now. But your happiness levels are still unstable because they depend on outward conditions. Are you healthy? Are you employed? How's your romantic life going? Because the factors of your life are constantly fluctuating, so is your happiness. Wouldn't it be great if you could be happy and stress-free no matter what?

Amazingly, there is a way. A path developed long ago by a man we call the Buddha, and refined over the last 2,500 years by Buddhist monks. Those funny-looking bald guys in orange robes actually figured out how to permanently end stress and slipped us the secret. The problem was the message was wrapped up in too much religious dogma, too many superstitions, and rules of celibacy so strict that most of us would refuse to listen. Consider this pearl of wisdom:

It would be better that your penis be stuck into the mouth of a black viper than into a woman's vagina. - The Buddha

I bet you never read that quote when you cracked open your fortune cookie. Even in Asian cultures, where many people are Buddhists, they are usually only nominally so.

They may go to a few temples, perform a few rituals, maybe even have a little meditation practice, but they never go all in on the business of actually ending stress. The path to the end of stress needs to be stripped of this cumbersome religious baggage, purged of its dubious metaphysical theories regarding karma and reincarnation, and translated into the language of contemporary science. That is what I present to you. Here is what I call Evolution and the 4 Noble Truths.

1. There is stress.

Stress here is defined as any sort of mental tension, from the slightest feeling of unease to all the way to depression and panic. It's anytime we are not totally freaking chill.

2. Stress is caused by desire.

When we normally think of the word "desire," we tend to imagine intense desires, like the desire to own a speedboat or pure sexual lust. Desire here is much more subtle. It is any sort of judgment about what is going on, and wishing it were different. Such as getting impatient while sitting at a red light. What will our impatience accomplish at that moment? If we look closely, we can see that these judgments occur during almost every single moment of conscious experience. They are built in to the way we process reality. The first two noble truths can be summed up as: *There is tension between what one wants, and what is.*

3. Stress can be eliminated by turning off the mechanisms in the brain that create desire.

The earliest organisms evolved mechanisms in their nervous system to approach food and mates, and to avoid being eaten. These early approach/avoidance mechanisms were the genesis of the more complicated system we have in our brains today. Still, all of the complex wants and emotions that we experience in everyday life can be simplified into two activities: Gravitating toward things that are good for the gene's ability to survive and replicate, and avoiding things that are harmful. If we were able to turn off the mechanism in our brain that causes us to perpetually judge our experience on the basis of approach or avoid, we would stop desire. And if we stopped desire, we would eliminate stress.

4. The way to turn off the mechanism in the brain that causes us to incessantly judge experience as something to approach or avoid is the use of meditation techniques that will ultimately change the way we process reality.

Harvard psychologist Daniel Brown, who also happens to be an advanced meditation instructor in the Mahamudra tradition of Tibetan Buddhism, sums it up like this:

If you look at your experience moment by moment, if the mind likes something, it moves towards that, to make more of it. If the mind doesn't like it, it moves away from that to make less of it. So incessantly the mind is moving towards things and moving away from things. It's reactive... It's built into how we process events moment by moment. And what these meditation practices do is minimize, and ultimately eradicate that reactivity. And if you eradicate that reactivity moment by moment so that it just doesn't occur, there is no basis for suffering.

Skeptic: Ok, I think I get it. If we eliminate desire, then we won't experience stress. But doesn't that mean we won't experience pleasure either? Doesn't happiness come from satisfying desires? Like: I'm hungry, so I eat a delicious steak. Or: I'm horny, so I plead with my wife to let this be the month we have sex.

A: I once wondered this too, so I asked Bhante G. He said it's perfectly fine to enjoy pleasures, a sunny day or a nice cup of tea as long as we don't crave them. The brain has different mechanisms for craving and enjoyment. That's why an addict can still crave his addiction long after he stops receiving pleasure from it.

Skeptic: So if we turn off this mechanism that creates desires, we won't just put an end to stress. But we will still be happy?

A: In Buddhist terminology, the state of having no desires is called nirvana, and it's the highest happiness you can imagine. In his wonderful book *Mindfulness, Bliss and Beyond* the Buddhist monk Ajahn Brahm tells the story of five children playing the wishing game. The child who came up with the best wish would win.

The first child wishes for some chocolate ice cream. The second child bests him by wishing for his own ice cream factory. That way he can have all the ice cream he wants. The third child goes even bigger, wishing for a billion dollars, that way not only could he own his own ice cream factory, but a candy factory, a toy factory and whatever else he could buy! The fourth child was a very clever girl, and instead of wishing for something material, she wishes for an unlimited amount of wishes. That way she could have the ice cream, the toy factory, the billion dollars and whatever else she wanted for the rest of her life! There was no way anyone was going to outdo her wish!

Then the fifth child, a shy boy, quietly said, "If I had a wish, I would wish to be so content that I wouldn't need any more wishes."

Up until now we have been content to function as what Dawkins called "the survival machines" for the gene's selfish desire to replicate into the next generation. We have been exemplary followers of our genetic overlords guidance, because as long as we successfully execute their plan, those genes will reward us with health and happiness. But, ironically, if we want to achieve the highest happiness of all, the bliss of perfect contentment, we have to transcend our genetic destiny. We have to change the way we process reality. We have to wake up.

What is Awakening?

Awakening is a cognitive change in how the brain perceives reality. This change leads to the diminishing and eventual cessation of desire. It usually doesn't happen all at once, but occurs incrementally as the subconscious processes special insights into the true nature of reality and how the mind works. The special insights that lead to Awakening are that all four of the following beliefs are false. Evolution programmed each of these beliefs into us not because they were true, but because they were beneficial to the replication of the genes residing inside us. For each of these false beliefs, I will tell you the truth, why evolution programmed us this way, and how the truth can set us free, with the traditional Buddhist term in parenthesis.

1. The Delusion: The world we see is objective reality.
The Truth: It's a highly filtered projection of our brains. (Emptiness)

Reality is merely an illusion. Albeit a very persistent one. - Albert Einstein

A wise man, recognizing the world is an illusion, does not act as if it is real, so he escapes the suffering. – Buddha

241

The world we see is very different from the objective reality that lies behind it. According to modern physics, our best model for the nature of the universe is quantum field theory. Everything in the universe is made up of fundamental forces and quantum particles. But when we look out at the world, do we see billions upon billions of elementary particles? When we look at water, do we see two hydrogen molecules and one oxygen molecule? No, we do not. We see a clear, liquid substance, suitable for drinking and bathing.

If our genes had evolved in different survival machines, as they do in other animals, our experience of the world would be vastly different. To understand this, just imagine reality from the point of view of an animal other than ourselves. Human beings can only see a tiny portion of the light spectrum. But some species of snakes -- boa constrictors, for example -- have pit organs on their heads that can sense heat in their surroundings, natural versions of infrared goggles. A snake does not have a sense of taste, but it smells with its tongue. Our ability to hear is rather pathetic compared to that of a dog, which can pick up sound waves far beyond what we can hear. A spider's experience of the world is even more foreign to us. Spiders and humans live in the same world, but because our sense organs are different we experience the world in a completely different way. Yet spiders and humans are still related; we are distant cousins. An alien species, unrelated to us in any way, may have an experience of reality so dramatically different from ours, that it would be beyond our comprehension to even imagine it. The world we see is not the objective world. It is a projection of our own minds.

<u>Why Evolution Programmed Us This Way</u>

Human beings take in the aspects of the world that our five senses can pick up, and filter that information through our brains. Our brain decides which pieces of information are useful for the purpose of survival and replication, and turns it all into an "output." That output is our conscious experience of the world. The world we experience is a product of our evolution, and what we see is what is highly relevant to our survival. When we look at a tiger, we see a large, powerful cat with sharp teeth who might eat us. We don't see trillions of tiny, vibrating strings of energy. Tigers are not objectively real. They are concepts produced by the brains of animals that can see them.

How the Truth Can Set Us Free

If the world that appears to us is a product of the mind, a dream-like reality created out of the quantum foam, how silly it is to become so attached to it. It is as if you are watching a movie. We know that the movie isn't real, yet we allow ourselves to put this aside and get caught up in the drama that is taking place on screen. We care for the characters, we feel joy when something good happens to them, and jump in fear when the killer suddenly appears brandishing a knife. If we were to snap out of this delusion and realize that we were sitting in a movie theater, watching nothing more than a bunch of pixels on a large screen change color, we would lose all our attachment to the characters and any outcome that befalls them. The same thing occurs when we realize that the world we see is mostly a creation of the mind, and is not objectively real.

Skeptic: Let's see if I've got this right. There is the outside world of quantum foam or strings of energy or whatever, and our brain takes in data from the senses and creates the reality that I see. This reality consists of trees, other people, cars, but most importantly -- my stress. Stress occurs when I take my ex-girlfriend to be this real person, and believe that my stories about not being able to live without her are real. After all, if my ex-girlfriend is just a bunch of quantum particles, and I am just a bunch of quantum particles, where is the suffering inherent in that? Stress is not an inherent part of the world; stress is the delusional creation of my own mind. If I am the creator of my own stress, because I desire objects that are not actually real, then it is possible for me to stop creating my own stress by no longer being so attached to this dream-like reality.

A: You got it.

2. The Delusion: The external world can satisfy us.
The Truth: As long as our minds interpret everything through the lens of desire, we will never be totally satisfied. (Dissatisfaction)

A friend of mine met a beautiful girl when he was 19. She was cute, sweet, fun, and she liked him back. It was not long before he was madly in love. But that summer his family had a week-long trip planned to the south of France. Before he met this girl, he'd been very excited about this trip; he loved to travel, had a fascination with French culture, and had even studied the language. So was he happy when he stepped into his luxury hotel room overlooking the beach with clear blue waters and battalions of topless women? Did he savor the fine cuisine and vintage wine? Was there a smile on his face as he biked around the cobbled streets and visited the ancient castles? No, he was miserable. He could not stand to be separated from his beloved for even an instant. He was half-a-world away from her gentle embrace, her lips, her laugh and her body. It was torture. His inner loneliness made him unable to enjoy the wonders of France.

To say that loneliness contaminates experience is not a groundbreaking idea. But I only gave you that example to set you up for the realization that all our experiences, not just trips to France when we are in love, are not completely satisfying. Even in those moments when we think we are at our happiest, we are not completely satisfied. Our greatest romance is tinted with moments of jealousy, anxiety, pain. The next time you are in the throes of passion, examine your mind. You might be surprised to find that even in the heat of the moment, there is a tinge of suffering. This would probably not be the time to blurt this out to your partner. But it's there. Because our brain is perpetually interpreting events moment by moment from the sense of attraction or avoidance, we will never totally be at ease.

Why Evolution Programmed Us This Way

If we believe that objects in the external world will actually bring us lasting satisfaction, like a pretty girlfriend or a degree from M.I.T., then we are more likely to try and obtain one, and that is good for our genes.

How the Truth Can Set Us Free

I once asked an expert meditator just how peaceful enlightenment was. He replied that I should imagine a moment in my life where I felt totally at ease. Maybe it was at the top of a mountain overlooking a great valley below. As your meditative skill progresses, everyday life will become just as peaceful. After you reach the early stages of enlightenment you will look back on the peace you felt on that mountaintop, and it will seem like absolute torment by comparison.

The Buddha taught us to be very dissatisfied with normal life. One might think: What a pessimist! But this is only because we haven't realized how much better we could have it. That's one reason it is advised to first reach jhana before beginning insight meditation practices. Once you have reached jhana -- a state of mind unhindered by mental afflictions -- and seen its enormous joy and bliss, the ordinary world simply can't compare. Even those experiences that we previously considered the most magnificent -- from a child being born to a four-hour Swedish massage -- are full of suffering relative to jhana.

As long as your mind is tainted by desire -- and it always is -- there is nothing you can do to be truly satisfied. It doesn't matter how rich we are, how many countries we visit, or how many beautiful people we make love to. We will never be completely satisfied as long as we are caught in the snares of attraction, aversion, delusion. There is only one thing to do. Purify our minds from desire.

3. The Delusion: That things we desire are permanent, and have the ability to bring about permanent happiness.
The Truth: Everything is impermanent. (Impermanence)

The Buddha noted that a major cause of suffering for people was their vain attempt to hold onto things that don't last. You meet someone and think that this initial love will last forever. You get a job that pays well and spend that money on a new car. Things are looking up! It's happiness from here on out -- until the relationship ends, your car breaks down, and your once steady income stream evaporates. We cling to these things, naively expecting them to stay the same, often in the face of logic and reason. We know damn well we are going to age, but when the inevitable wrinkles form around our eyes, and the hairs on our head take on a silver hue, we still get upset and reach for the tweezers.

Why Evolution Programmed Us This Way

If we hold on to the delusion that love will last forever, it might actually make us more attractive to potential mates. You are far more likely to get laid on your wedding night after a vow that includes "till death do us part" than if you recited the words: "I'll marry you, but there's a greater than 50 percent chance that we are going to get divorced and end up hating each other. Probably within a decade."

How the Truth Can Set Us Free

When we understand that everything in this universe is impermanent, we stop clinging to things we hoped would never change. We become more comfortable with the fact that our relationships will end, that we will grow old and eventually die. We realize that change is inevitable, so we stop fighting it, and just accept it. When we accept it, we become totally attuned to the true nature of the universe: that everything is constantly changing, so we no longer get stressed out when it inevitably does. It is only through false expectations of how the world works that people get disappointed. There is a story about one ancient stoic philosopher who managed to remain free from grief despite the death of his son. When asked how he accomplished this, he responded, "I never believed my son to be immortal."

4. Delusion: There is a conscious self.
The Truth: There is no conscious self. (No-self)

And now we come to the commonly misunderstood concept of "no-self". This is both the most difficult and most important concept to understand in all of contemplative tradition. The idea that what we think of as "I" is just an illusion. This idea is going to need its own chapter.

No-Self

Skeptic: No-self? Are you kidding me? Are you telling me that I don't exist?

A: What is it that you think you are?

Skeptic: Do you see me? Look at me; I am this body. This brain! Think about what you just said. What is it that *you* think *you* are? Why would you use the word *you* if there was no *I* to hear you?

A: The terms "you" and "I" are being used here as a convenience or a convention. It's the same way that we always refer to the river Thames by the same name, acting as if it is a stable, unchanging entity, when it is not. Heraclitus pointed out thousands of years ago that you cannot step into the same river twice. The waters that flow through the river are constantly changing. Similarly, the cells in your body are constantly being replaced; physically you are not the same person you were before. Yet for the sake of convenience, I still refer to you as "you".

Skeptic: How about this: I am whatever it is that has experiences. I am the thing that feels, I am the thing that thinks. There can't be thoughts without a thinker!

A: Oh, no? Let me tell you the story of Bahiya. Back in the time of the Buddha, a ship was a-sail in the Indian waters when it sprang a leak. All the men on board died and became food for the fishes and tortoises.

Skeptic: Tortoises? Seriously?

A: Yeah, I don't know, but that's how the story goes. Just roll with me here. I'm about to get to the good part.

Skeptic: Ok. Get to it.

A: So all the men died except for one, Bahiya, who managed to seize a plank, and, holding on for dear life, was able to float safely to a nearby port. When he reached land, he was completely naked, so for lack of any better clothing material, he made himself a garment out of twigs and bark. He found himself a begging bowl, and having nothing to eat, went around town seeking alms. The people in the city, seeing his ascetic appearance, figured that he must be a noble mystic. So they filled his bowl with food and treated him with reverence. "This life is pretty good," thought Bahiya, and he continued his new career as a fake guru.

People offered him expensive robes to replace the bark he was wearing, but he refused. "He must be a great saint!" thought the people, and his fame grew. Being treated with such respect, Bahiya came to believe that he was someone special. Then one day a deva (an angel-like figure) that wished nothing but wellness for Bahiya came to him and said: "Bahiya, you are not an arahant (a fully enlightened being). If you want to be one you must go and find the Buddha at Savatthi."

Bahiya traveled straight through the night and arrived in Savatthi the next day. When he got there, the Buddha was on his alms round. Although weary from his journey, Bahiya had a keen sense of urgency. He had to see the Buddha immediately. After all, life is fickle, and anyone can be killed at an instant. What horrible luck it would be if Bahiya or the Buddha were to die before he could learn the Buddha's teachings. So he went looking for the Buddha. After finding the sage, he threw himself at his feet and asked to hear what the great teacher had to say.

"You have come at a bad time, Bahiya," said the Buddha. "I am on my alms round. You will have to wait until later." Bahiya again begged to be taught, but still the Buddha rebuffed him. He saw that Bahiya was too excited just to be in his presence. If he taught him now, in this excited state, Bahiya would not be able to comprehend what was said to him. He had to make him wait a little. Finally, after Bahiya begged him for a third time, explaining that it was a dangerous world, that they could die at any moment, the Buddha relented and offered up the following bit of wisdom:

"Then, Bāhiya, you should train yourself thus: In reference to the seen, there will be only the seen. In reference to the heard, only the heard. In reference to the sensed, only the sensed. In reference to the cognized, only the cognized. That is how you should train yourself. When for you there will be only the seen in reference to the seen, only the heard in reference to the heard, only the sensed in reference to the sensed, only the cognized in reference to the cognized, then, Bāhiya, there is no you in connection with that. When there is no you in connection with that, there is no you there. When there is no you there, you are neither here nor yonder nor between the two. This, just this, is the end of stress."

Right then and there, Bahiya understood completely and became fully enlightened. "May I join your order of monks?" Bahiya asked? "First, go and find yourself a robe," replied the Buddha, who then left to continue his alms round.

A few moments later Bahiya was gored by a cow and died.

Skeptic: Good story. But clearly I am not as gifted as Bahiya. For I have just heard the exact words that he heard and yet I am not enlightened. Would you mind running what the Buddha said by me again.

A: No problem. You began by saying that whatever you are, it is that which sees, that which hears, and that which thinks.

Skeptic: Check.

A: When the Buddha says that in the seen there is just the seen, in the heard there is just the heard, he denies that very claim. There is not someone who hears, there is just hearing. There is not someone who sees, there is just seeing. There is not someone who thinks, there is just thinking. That which is taken to be "you" is really just the collection of these aggregates. There is no separate "you" apart from the thinking, hearing, seeing, feeling, etc.

Skeptic: Ok, but I'm not going to take the Buddha's word for it. What do scientists have to say about this?

A: Scientists are in total agreement. Here is Harvard cognitive psychologist Steven Pinker on the illusion of "I":

"Another startling conclusion from the science of consciousness is that the intuitive feeling we have that there's an executive "I" that sits in a control room of our brain, scanning the screens of the senses and pushing the buttons of the muscles, is an illusion. Consciousness turns out to consist of a maelstrom of events distributed across the brain. These events compete for attention, and as one process outshouts the others, the brain rationalizes the outcome after the fact, and concocts the impression that a single self was in charge all along."

There have been a host of studies to support this. There is simply no "ghost in the machine." That feeling you have that there is a specific "me" is just another feeling arising in your consciousness. It is just another thought that pops up in the field of awareness. It is not a thing that experiences the other objects of consciousness, but just another object of consciousness itself.

Skeptic: What do you mean when you say that the self is just another object of consciousness?

A: We tend to think consciousness works the following way: We have a brain, and that brain produces a self, which in turn *has* thoughts, feelings, memories, etc.

Brain > Self > Thoughts, Feelings, Memories, Etc.

But in reality we have a brain that produces thoughts, feelings, memories, and a *sense* of self, etc. This sense of self *doesn't have* thoughts, feelings, and memories, it is just another collection of thoughts and feelings produced by the brain, and has no special status above other thoughts and feelings.

Brain > Thoughts, Feelings, Memories, Sense of Self, Etc.

Skeptic: I think I understand intellectually. But I still feel as if there is a me! I still feel as if "I" am the one who is thinking.

A: Let's play a game. Let's see if we can get your conscious self to think of something. Sound easy? Okay quick! Think of an animal! What popped into your head? For me it was a penguin. What about you? Now why did you choose that animal and not some other animal? How did you come up with that particular animal? Did it just pop into your head? And you aren't really sure why? 'Who' chose that animal? Was it a conscious 'you'? Or did it pop into consciousness from the subconscious?

Now just watch your thoughts, and see what thoughts come up. Where did they come from? Who chose those thoughts? Did you choose them? Or did they simply arise from the subconscious?

Play around with this, and tell me if you can get your consciousness to come up with any thought. Or do these thoughts always arise from the subconscious? If they always bubble up from the subconscious, what does that say about the idea that there is a conscious self that thinks?

One of the meditations used to see no-self has the meditator examining each aspect of his experience and then asking "Is this 'me'? Is the sound I hear 'me'?" Certainly not. Is this feeling of anger 'me'?" Is the thought that pops up and then quickly vanishes 'me'?" Eventually, the meditator gets so good at it that he can ask questions such as "Is this awareness 'me'?" "Is this intention 'me'?" One by one, the meditator knocks down the potential candidates for "me" until there is nothing left. When one has gone looking for the "I" and found that it is not there, the feeling that there is an "I" fades away.

Skeptic: It fades away? How is that possible?

A: Have you ever been in a situation where you had a false belief, and this belief caused you to feel a certain way? Then, when you realized that your belief was false, this feeling evaporated? Let me give an example. One year on April 1st, my brother, who was in the midst of an action-packed adventure in New Zealand, wrote my mother a short email explaining that he had hurt himself in a bungee jump accident. The cord was too long, and my brother had slammed into the ground breaking his spine. He was now paralyzed from the waist down. My mother, being a fairly neurotic person, worked herself into a such a panic as she read all of this that she fainted, fell out of her chair and collapsed on the ground before she could ever get to the bottom of the email that read "April Fool's; I'm fine!"

Finally, after coming to, my mother read the rest of the email and realized her belief that my brother was now paralyzed was false, and subsequently her feeling of horror evaporated. Similarly, when the meditator sees through direct experience that the idea of a separate self, a thinker of thoughts, an experiencer of experience, is but an illusion, then the corresponding feeling of there being a self will also evaporate.

Skeptic: How can you function without a conscious self? How can you 'know' anything, or 'do' anything?

A: You never had a conscious self to begin with! You only had the false notion and feeling that you had one. So you can still do all the same things as before. You can still

255

go to work, you can still interact with other people, you can still do your taxes. To understand why, you have to know a little bit about how neuroscientists and cognitive psychologists think the brain and consciousness operate.

How Consciousness Works

The brain is actually divided into dozens of subconscious modules that each perform specific tasks. These include visual modules, auditory modules, thinking modules, emotional modules, and a narrative spinner -- a module that sort of sums up what is going on in the brain and concocts a story. The important point here is that all of these modules do their work subconsciously and then project their results into consciousness. Consciousness can be thought of as a screen that other subconscious modules can then "see" to gather information. In this case, instead of consciousness being a "do-er" or "thinker," consciousness is more like a community bulletin board or information exchange, where various subconscious modules can learn what the other modules are up to.

To give an example, when you think "I'm hungry," what is really going is that one subconscious module decides the body needs nourishment and projects that result into consciousness in the form of a feeling of hunger, so that another subconscious module can "see" that result and then take action. Perhaps the memory module gets activated and comes to the conclusion "I have leftovers in the fridge," and projects that information into consciousness, which then gets seen by modules in charge of movement. It is these modules that cause you to get up and walk to the kitchen.

At no moment during this quest to get food was there a conscious self making a decision. All the decisions were made by the various subconscious modules. The function of consciousness is merely to integrate these distinct subconscious modules.

Skeptic: So if there is no conscious self making decisions, or doing much of anything, why is everyone under the illusion that there is?

A: Let me explain.

Why Evolution Programmed Us This Way

Humans evolved in social groups, and it is the social nature of our species that gave us the illusion of a sense of self. Within our tribe we had to distinguish between different members: Who was a potential mate, who wasn't, who was a friend, who were our enemies. We gave each other names, we developed the use of the pronouns "You" and "I." We would plan for future actions by imaging ourselves in future scenarios. *What will I do the next time Bonga steals my grapes?* Somewhere along the way we got confused into thinking that these pronouns referred to some substance within our skulls that was the conscious self. We then developed egos around this idea of being a self, an image of ourselves that we needed to monitor and constantly critique. *Am I well liked? Am I funny? Should I have said that?* These self-referential thought patterns proved useful at augmenting our social status within the tribe, and hence our ability to replicate our genes.

How the Truth Can Set Us Free

I asked Bhante G why getting rid of the sense of self was beneficial. "Well, I'll tell you," he smiled. "It makes you a lot more humble." He then paused for effect. "I could be sitting up here thinking: Look at me! I am so wise! I have to teach you fools everything!" We all laughed.

For most people, self-referential narratives are usually not about how great we are, but about how we aren't satisfied with ourselves and need to impress other people. The most striking thing I've noticed from being around enlightened people is that I get no sense that they care one way or another what I think about them. Not in the sense of "These guys don't give a fuck what I think." In fact, It's exactly the opposite; they tend to exude compassion and benevolence. But they aren't self-conscious. They're totally comfortable with themselves.

Self-referential narratives were an adaptation that proved beneficial in passing on our genes, but these narratives remove us from the peacefulness of the present moment. With the desire to maintain a certain image of ourselves, we turn on that mechanism in our brain that constantly judges our behavior in terms of approach (the image we like about ourselves) or avoidance (the image we don't like about ourselves). Whenever our ego is challenged, we suffer. *How dare that jerk think that about me!* Whenever we aren't living up to our own standards, we suffer. *I'm a failure, I'll never be successful, I'm an idiot, how the fuck did I lose to Trump?* It's amazing how much time we spend ruminating.

When we realize that that we aren't a conscious self, we lose our attachments to our thoughts and the stories they weave. Thoughts come up, and then they go, feelings come up, and then they go, but we don't get attached to them. We don't think: These are *my* thoughts, *my* feelings. When seen objectively, these thoughts and feelings don't have the same emotional pull. They may arise, but they don't proliferate. They come and they go.

Meditators report that the relaxation that comes from dropping these self-referential narratives is like taking off a heavy backpack after a long hike. There is a wonderful sense of relief that you no longer have to deal with all the bullshit you have been carrying around in your mind all day long. These narratives cause a great deal of stress, perhaps even most of our stress. The Buddha once compared the amount of stress alleviated when getting rid of the false sense of self to the size of a mountain. While the amount of stress that remained was only a few pebbles.

Insight Meditation

Now you know the four special insights of Awakening. So why don't you feel very enlightened? For the same reason you can't read a book about basketball and then go out to your neighborhood court and shoot like Stephen Curry. Awakening isn't a theoretical knowledge, it's a procedural one. We need to practice. We have to change the way our subconscious interprets reality. We have to get it into our heads, deep within the crevices of our skulls, somewhere amongst that gooey web of neurons and synapses, that the world we see is a subjective model of reality produced by our brains. Nothing within it, not the people, not the objects, not our ideals and ideas, not even ourselves, are worth clinging on to.

How Awakening Happens in the Brain

During our normal, distracted state of mind, the various subconscious modules in the brain compete for attention. One module will go, "Hey I feel like eating chocolate cake," and another will reply, "No, remember, we are trying to eat Paleo!" Eventually, one wins out; and since you have been reading this book, hopefully it's the latter. But when we are in a deep state of concentration, our subconscious modules become unified towards a common goal. This unification means that instead of bickering among each other, the subconscious modules will be attentive and receptive to any insights we might have. This allows our new insights to penetrate down into the subconscious and bring about the radical change in the way we process reality. Awakening happens when we combine very deep concentration (one should be able to reach jhana) with lots of deep insight. We've already learned how to practice concentration, but how do we "practice" insight?

The Practice

The first people to Awaken did so by accident. Shinzen Young, the meditation teacher who has spent time with native tribes, theorizes that some shamans may have stumbled upon enlightenment after a lifetime of getting themselves into deep states of trance and developing equanimity (having neither approach nor avoidance reactions) towards the grueling physical toll of many day healing rituals.

The Buddha's great contribution is that he may have been the first to figure out a systematic way to enlightenment. There are many ways of doing insight practice within Buddhism. In the Tibetan tradition of *Mahamudra,* the student describes his experiences to the teacher and the teacher in turn points out insights to the student, asking: "Have you looked at it like this?" In Zen, the teacher asks the student nonsensical questions called koans to pop the student out his conceptual way of thinking. Questions such as: "What is the color of the wind?" When the student inevitably gets the answer wrong, the master hits him with a stick. If he gets it wrong twice, the master cuts his nuts off.

Just making sure you are still paying attention.

I am not a Tibetan lama, nor do I have a stick to beat you with, so instead I'll refer you to a practice called "noting." It has the advantages of simple instructions and can be practiced by yourself, anywhere at anytime, which allows you to make gains very quickly.

The Technique

As when doing concentration practice, start by following the inhalation and exhalation of the breath. Do this for a little while until your mind settles down and you feel calm and focused. Distractions will come up, but instead of ignoring them and returning to the breath as we did before, switch your focus to the distraction, say a thought, and note "thinking." A pain in the knee comes up, note "pain," a tingling sensation, note "tingling." If you notice something in your visual field, "seeing." Do not worry about being exact with your words, nor should you try to note more than one thing at a time. Just apply a general label, say it once or twice, drop it and move on to the next sensation that occurs. If after noting something and nothing else comes up, then return to the breath until the next distraction appears.

This technique also has the advantage of being able to be practiced all day long, which is especially helpful while on retreat. As you get up from your cushion and go about the day, the noting practice continues. Note "standing," "walking", "turning", "chewing", "seeing", "lifting". The idea is to maintain a constant and vigilant meta-level awareness to all your activities.

There is debate among meditators whether one needs to label each note by silently saying "thinking," "feeling," etc., or if you can just be aware of thinking without needing to label it with a word. Again, as in most things involving meditation, experiment with both and see what is best for you. Most practitioners find labeling each distraction with a silent word useful, at least until concentration is very strong, at which point the sensations are so fine, and come so fast, that it is best not to bother with labeling, just mentally take notice.

By noting each sensation, you are training your mind to realize impermanence, dissatisfaction, and no-self. When you note "feeling," and then watch it vanish, you are noticing the impermanence of that feeling. You realize that this feeling can't possibly bring lasting satisfaction, and is hence, unsatisfactory. As you note all the various parts of the body and mental stream, you realize that none of these sensations are you. What you thought was a single, permanent self is really just a bundle of vibrating thoughts, feelings and sensations. When you realize the impermanence, dissatisfaction, and no-self in all the phenomena that make up experiential reality, you realize the futility in grasping on to them. You let go. You relax. You become free.

Skeptic: Ok, so if I master these concentration and insight practices, I will eventually Awaken. But how will I know when that happens? Is there a specific moment when I can declare that I am Awakened?

A: All the meditative traditions have their own criteria for Awakening, and they rarely agree with each other. This is because Awakening exists on a continuum. Any attempt to draw a line in the sand and say, "Now, I am Awakened" is purely conceptual. What's more important is to notice how over the course of time that your approach and avoidance mechanisms have dialed down, that you are more content with reality to be just as it is, and that your stress levels have dropped. Whether anyone has ever *fully* Awakened, that is completely eliminated all forms of mentally created stress, I am agnostic about. But what is possible is to reduce your stress levels and achieve a sense of deep peace far beyond what you ever thought possible.

Skeptic: That sounds real nice and all, but I don't know man. I'm still unsure about this. The part about losing your sense of self, that sounds a bit scary! I'm just not sure it's worth it!

A: Awakening does not come without the price of admission. You will stop caring so much about the things you are currently so passionate about. You may even have odd experiences in your meditation that will be unnerving. It can be scary to truly let go, although once you do, you will realize there was nothing to fear. Some meditators have described this feeling as jumping off a cliff, only to realize they could fly. Still, having a teacher to guide you through any potential rough patches, to bounce questions off of, to help elucidate the nuances of the path is highly recommended.

You won't fully get over these doubts until you see the benefits from first hand experience. Right now, you might even doubt that Awakening is desirable. This is normal. People have had these doubts for thousands of years. Doubts that the writers of the *suttas* tried to quell with this legendary parable about the Buddha.

Once, there was a young monk named Nanda who one day went up to the Buddha and said, "I'm done with the Holy life, I want to return to being a normal person." The Buddha asked why, and the young monk said that he had met a girl from Sakya, the most beautiful in the land, with long flowing hair.

Just then the Buddha grabbed the young monk by the arm, and they magically left the world they were in and flew to a heavenly realm where there were 500 pink-footed nymphs. "What do you think young monk? Are these 500 pink-footed nymphs more alluring than that girl from Sakya, the prettiest in the land?" asked the Buddha.

"Revered sir, compared to these 500 pink-footed nymphs, that Sakyan girl, the loveliest in the land, is like a mutilated she-monkey that has had its ears and nose chopped off. She does not count; she is not worth a fraction compared to them; there is no comparison. These 500 nymphs are far more beautiful, more fair to behold, and more alluring."

"Rejoice, Nanda, rejoice, Nanda! I guarantee that you will obtain 500 pink-footed nymphs if you follow my instructions."

"If, revered sir, the Lord guarantees that I will obtain 500 pink-footed nymphs, I shall be content in living the holy life under the Lord."

Nanda practiced and practiced hoping to get those 500 nymphs. Then one day, after some very intense practice Nanda reached a state where he felt so content, that the present moment was just perfect as it was. Nothing could make it any better. He went to the Buddha and told him that his mind was now taintless and that the Buddha no longer had to uphold his promise to give him 500 nymphs, as he had no desire for them anymore.

Skeptic: Ok, I get it, Awakening is better than being rich. It's better than the high of a drug. It's better than having a harem of 500 pink-footed nymphs. And not only does Awakening feel better than these worldly pleasures, it's stable. I can lose my job, get divorced, develop elephantiasis and still be happy. If all this is true, to live my life in any other way would be madness.

VI. INTEGRATION

<u>Fusion</u>

The *homo sapiens* animal is a handful of stardust that has become conscious of itself, a fact more incredible than all the creation myths of the ancient religions. Within us, we have a genetic program, complete with desires, emotional reactions, pleasures and pains -- all united in the task of getting microscopic strands of DNA to fuse with one another, and then repeat the process when the next generation comes of age. When we follow our genetic blueprint, we are one of the lucky species that will experience happiness.

But modern life is so vastly different from the environment in which our genes originally evolved that our bodies' response to the social isolation, traffic, bills, long working hours, concrete jungles and lack of meaning has placed our body in a state of chronic stress. Constantly on edge, we are quick to anger, to feel anxiety and worry. We become depressed, we don't sleep well. To combat our lack of sleep, we intake stimulants to give us energy and then drink booze to take the edge off. The natural insouciance of the human animal is gone. Yet not all hope is lost. By taking a multi-faceted approach, we can turn off this perpetual stress signal and return to the carefree ways of our ancestors.

We have to tackle the environmental stressors on our body and return to a nutritional and movement lifestyle reminiscent of our ancestors. By feeding our bodies a healthy diet of nutritious whole foods, complete with fresh fruits and vegetables, and heaps of quality meats, we are giving our body the fuel it needs to function well. Most importantly, we will avoid the disease, depression, and inability to focus that results from dopamine depletion. And dopamine depletion is caused by sugary, processed foods.

We must remain vigilant against the inactivity, sitting, lethargy and passive entertainment that contemporary culture tries to force upon us. We need to run around in the sun, lift heavy things, and move in agile ways until our hearts thump in our chest and we high-five our teammates in victory. By doing this, our bodies will be fit, lithe, sexy and disease free.

All this activity calls for rest, and it is vitally important that we get quality sleep. So many of us don't adhere to the circadian rhythms that our mammalian bodies have adapted to over the course of millions of years. We shouldn't need to take sleeping pills to pass out or drink copious amounts of caffeine to wake up. It is possible to fall asleep naturally in a relaxing slumber and awaken with the energy needed for the pursuits of the day.

The songs of birds, the rustling of leaves, the soothing sounds of a flowing creek. For thousands of generations this was the soundtrack to our lives. Today, it has been replaced by the stress-producing cacophony of car horns, jackhammers, police sirens. We must make frequent escapes from the smog and pollution, out into the fresh air of natural habitats. Turn off the cell phone. Leave the iPad at home and trek into the wilderness. Splash around in the streams, breathe in the aroma of the forest. Notice how the act of disconnecting yourself from the constant barrage of texts, emails, tweets and Facebook updates gives you a sense of peace and calm. Your batteries will be recharged, your focus will improve. Deep down inside, your body knows that you are a large primate and that the wild is your true home.

We have to reconnect to the tribe. So many people today feel lonely, isolated, lacking the deep communal bonds that united our tribal ancestors. Many of the positive emotions we experience today evolved to facilitate cooperative relationships between people. We should make an effort to improve our relationships with family members, to spend more time with friends, and join groups of people that will influence us in positive ways. That could be your local CrossFit box, a dance group, or a Buddhist *sangha*. Even Buddhist monks, who are often thought to be solitary loners, prefer the company of like-minded friends. One day Ananda, the Buddha's first cousin and one of his most respected disciples, sat down next to the Buddha and said: "This is half of the holy life, Lord: admirable friendship, admirable companionship, admirable camaraderie."

The Buddha looked at his cousin, and replied: "Don't say that, Ananda. Don't say that. Admirable friendship, admirable companionship, admirable camaraderie is actually the *whole* of the holy life."

If we were to do just these five things -- eat right, get fit, sleep well, be in nature, and develop good relationships -- there is a good chance that we would live happy and healthy lives. Of course, we would not be immune to things that are beyond our control, and we could never perfectly recreate the environmental conditions of the original hunter-gatherer lifestyle. We need more tools if we hope to live as placidly, as fully in the present, existential moment as they did. This is where mind training comes in.

The first step is to break away from our habitually negative thought patterns. Instead of obsessing over every little setback or roadblock, we will learn to find the silver lining. We will learn to think rationally and adopt the motto: "If there is a solution to the problem, there is no need to worry, and if there is no solution to the problem, worrying won't solve it – so why bother worrying?" We will accept the positivity challenge and refuse to rest until we have succeeded. From there, we will work on calming and focusing our mind with concentration meditation exercises. We will do metta practices to develop a mind that is more compassionate, joyful and infused with benevolent goodwill. We will refine our attention until we achieve the states of jhana -- a natural ecstasy without side effects -- that is available to us whenever we decide to sit down on the cushion.

Finally, we will do insight meditation to examine the nature of conscious experience more accurately. We will discover experientially how our beliefs that we are a separate self, that things are permanent, and that things will satisfy us are mere delusions that cause suffering. We will realize the emptiness of phenomena by seeing that the world we cling to so passionately is at best a highly filtered projection of the mind; and with this we will stop wanting the world to be any different than it is. From then on, we will live in sublime peace.

This is the path laid out in this book. For ultimate well-being, we need to fuse the paleolithic lifestyle with Buddhist meditation. One without the other is incomplete. Without meditation, the modern person living a paleo lifestyle will never experience the profound joy and insight of the serious meditation practitioner. On the other hand, someone who solely meditates won't have the physical health and vitality of one who exercises, sleeps and eats the paleo way. One of the most respected Tibetan Buddhist masters of the last century, Tulku Urgyen Rinpoche, suffered from diabetes. Other highly enlightened folks I've talked to have mentioned that they could be happier if their jobs allowed them a more natural sleep cycle or if they exercised more. Awakening does not mean that your mammalian body has become immune to biological stressors. It is with the fusion of a paleo lifestyle and Buddhist meditation that we can become as happy and healthy as humanly possible.

This Short, Precious Life

The vast majority of people who buy this book will not make it past the first chapters. If you are one of the minority, one of those people who have read through and made it to the finale, I congratulate you. Still, most of you will finish this book, set it down and go on living your lives just as you lived them before. That is why I am ending this book about health and happiness with an important reminder: You are going to die.

If you are lucky, it will be decades from now when you finally slip away peacefully in your sleep. If you are unlucky, you could find out that you have terminal cancer tomorrow. Or you might be on your way to work when a teenager smashes her SUV into you because her text "OMG...cutest cat picture eva" simply couldn't wait. Death can happen in an instant.

If you were to die today, how would you feel about your life?

Close your eyes and visualize yourself on your deathbed. You lie there underneath the white sheets, draped in a hospital gown with an IV in your arm. A doctor has told you that you only have a few hours to live. Looking back on your life, do you have any regrets? When

273

this day comes, and it will, do you want to be able to look back, smile contently and think, "I made the most of it."

In Tibetan Buddhism, awareness of death is considered the very first step on the path to enlightenment. The point of this daunting reminder is to motivate you to drop all the trivial bullshit you spend so much time on and use your life to do something that will make you truly happy. The 11th-century master Gampopa wrote:

In the beginning, you should be pursued by the fear of death like a deer escaping from a trap. In the middle, you should have nothing to regret, even if you die at this moment, like a peasant who has worked his land with care. In the end, you should be happy, like someone who has completed an immense task... The most important thing to know is that there is no time to lose, as if an arrow had hit a vital spot in your body.

Wasted Time

Around 49 A.D, Seneca wrote a letter to his friend Paulinus entitled "The Brevity of Life." He argued that the trouble with life was not that it was so short, but that we wasted so much of it. Some people waste time trying to quench an insatiable greed, others toiling at jobs they despise. Some people destroy themselves with alcohol or drugs. Then there are the fickle types, hopping from one activity to another, always starting new projects but never finishing any. Others have no plans at all, and simply let fate decide their course.

How much of life do we really live? Take a look at your average day. How much of it is filled with fun and joy? Think of all the chores you do, from brushing your teeth to commuting, to working, to grocery shopping, to cleaning, to errands. Fall asleep, wake up, repeat the cycle. Before you know it, the year is over, the wrinkles on your face have become more pronounced, your belly has doubled in size, and the sand in your hourglass of life continues to trickle away.

Much of adult life is devoted to routine chores, and I have no foolproof solution for building more free time into your life. What I do believe is that our free time is so precious that we cannot waste it being click-bait monkeys, burrowing down into that sinkhole of internet articles and mindless television shows.

Stop that nonsense now. Not only is it a waste of time, but the internet is rewiring your brain to expect instant gratification. You have lost your ability to be patient. The endless quest for the next stimulus that is going to deliver the slightest dopamine rush is no way to live your life. We must guard our time as if it were the most precious treasure. For that is exactly what life is: a rare gift between an eternity of nothingness.

Oh, How Lucky You Are!

Consider how improbable it is that you are even alive. Each and every one of us started out as one of millions of sperm cells in our father's ejaculation. That one sperm cell survived and fertilized our mother's egg. If she had been lying in a different position at the moment of climax, a different sperm cell would have crossed the finish line and someone else would have been born. Not only that, think how fortuitous it is that our parents are human beings, when the far more likely scenario would have resulted in our being born as beetles. The odds against us ever being born are astronomical, yet here we are. In order to appreciate this, one of the first meditations that young Tibetan practitioners are advised to do is to imagine being a cow. Picture yourself having four legs, being covered in dung and flies, eating grass. Mooing. After doing this, they contrast being a cow with all the freedoms you enjoy as a human. Going back and forth between imagining being a cow and imagining that they are human, they learn to bask in the good fortune of being a person.

If you had been born a European peasant in the middle ages, the vast wisdom of Eastern philosophy and evolutionary psychology would have been unknown to you. Even if you had been born in the United States in the early 20th century, these teachings would still have been unavailable. Most people on earth today will live lives of endless drudgery, working in factories for a few dollars a day. That is the only life they will ever know. They have no one to teach them about the freedom that is possible. They are too busy making your smartphone.

If you have made it this far into the book, you probably have sufficient health and intelligence to allow you to practice meditation and commune with nature. You could have been born mentally handicapped. You could have contracted some illness that left you demented. You could have been dropped on your head as a child. There are also those who suffer from physical disabilities that don't allow them to engage in the thrilling athletic activities those of us with able bodies can enjoy. But even if you are one of these people, do not despair! Almost everyone can still benefit from sport and meditation.

In the 1960s, thousands of Westerners flocked to India to meet meditation masters, braving the long journey and the inevitable Montezuma's Revenge, Himalayan version. This is what you had to do if you wanted to find yourself in the company of someone enlightened, because such sages were not to be found outside of the Asian land mass. A few centuries ago, the situation was even more dire. To get to

Asia, you had to trek on foot (either your own, or on the back of a large animal) over mountains, rivers, deserts, across whole continents to reach such a person. And once you arrived, you probably had no way to assess the character of these masters, whether they were wise men or charlatans. Nowadays, many of the masters from the East have traveled to the West and have trained their own western-born students in the art of meditation. With just a bit of research, you can go and find a meditation master to give you personal instructions, either locally or through Skype.

How grateful we should be for the geniuses of the past! If Siddhartha Guatama, the man who would come to be known as the Buddha, had contracted pneumonia as a child and died, the path to Awakening may never have been discovered. We are actually lucky that he even decided to teach what he knew. After attaining enlightenment, the Buddha debated whether or not to teach what he had learned to others. He felt that humans were too polluted by greed, ignorance and hatred to ever recognize the path to enlightenment. He wondered if he would be wasting his time and energy explaining such esoteric concepts to people so cloaked in darkness. Luckily for all of us, his friend Sahampati convinced him that there are those out there with only a little dust in their eyes, and at least some of them would be able to understand the teachings. Remember also that the Buddha himself had teachers that taught him the preliminary meditative techniques that were being passed around the Indian subcontinent. We all stand on the shoulders of giants. Even Buddha.

And what of Charles Darwin? Where would our understanding of human nature be without his trip to the Galapagos? And what of the anthropologists who braved malaria and man-eating tigers and anacondas, and risked getting eaten by cannibals, all to bring us the surprising truth about the natives' cheerful lives.

The impossible odds against you sitting where you are right now, reading this book, are too enormous to fathom. Who told you about this book's existence? What if you had never met that person? What if the printing press had never been invented hundreds of years ago? What if the comet that struck the Yucatan Peninsula 65 million years ago had a trajectory just fractions of a degree different? Dinosaurs would still roam the planet, and hairy apes like us would never have evolved.

But here you are. A conscious *homo sapiens,* with the tools, abilities, and resources at your disposal to live in a way that is happy and healthy. Life need not be a struggle filled with worry, anxieties, anger, boredom. It is not difficult to have a body that is fit, athletic and sexy, provided you are willing to change your diet and commit yourself to exercising. By setting aside a period of the day to meditate you can greatly reduce stress, and even bliss out to a degree you didn't previously think possible. Sadly, most people won't make the time to do so. Don't be one of these people. Instead, have the courage to break free from the stupefying, unsatisfactory lifestyle of passive entertainment and consumerism to enjoy a richer life, the one your human body evolved for.

How to Feel Alive

You need to embrace the fact that you are a wild animal. I want you to run through the forest barefoot and shirtless until your heart races and you are out of breath. I want you to jump through a waterfall and cool off in a natural swim hole. I want you to pick ripe berries off a tree and place them in a pretty girl's mouth. I want you to learn how to hunt, skin and cook your own food over the campfire as you laugh with your friends until your belly aches. I want you to sing, dance and gyrate your hips with uncontrollable passion. I want you to paint your body and consummate your lust in an erotic ritual. I want you to look up at the canopy of stars and lose yourself in the incomprehensible enormity of the universe.

And meditate, my friends, you must meditate! Experience the sublime peace of the unperturbed mind, the ecstasy of jhana. And then, perhaps, one day, the highest happiness of all, nirvana. But you must get started now, with the same urgency as if your hair were on fire. Remember -- You are going to die.

The Evening Gatha (a zen chant)

Let me respectfully remind you,
Life and death are of supreme importance.
Time swiftly passes by and opportunity is lost.
Each of us should strive to awaken. . .awaken,
Take heed. Do not squander your life.

The End

Further Info

For further info, including workouts, diet plans, personal consulting and more, visit www.thetribalway.com

<u>Acknowledgments</u>

Thank you to my family, my dad, my mom, and my siblings. This book took years to write, and I know that deep down you all thought I'd never finish it. But you supported me anyway. You have no idea how much that means.

And a special thanks to Joe Queenan. Why an author of his immense stature would take time out of his busy schedule to edit my book is a complete mystery. He must be working on a sequel to *My Goodness*.

And thank you to all the scientists, philosophers, psychologists and anthropologists who came before me. We all stand on the shoulders of giants and I could have never written this book without your works.

References

Books

Brahm, Ajahn. *Mindfulness, Bliss, and Beyond: A Meditator's Handbook.* Boston: Wisdom Publications, 2006. Print.

Brody, H. (2001). *The Other Side of Eden.* North Point Press.

Diamond, Jared M. *The World until Yesterday: What Can We Learn from Traditional Societies?* New York: Viking, 2012. Print.

Dowman, Keith, and Sonam Paljor. *The Divine Madman.* London: Rider, 1980. Print.

Duffy, Kevin. *Children of the Forest.* New York: Dodd, Mead, 1984. Print.

Eliade, Mircea, and Willard R. Trask. *Shamanism: Archaic Techniques of Ecstasy.* New York: Bollingen Foundation; Distributed by Pantheon, 1964. Print.

Everett, Daniel Leonard. *Don't Sleep, There Are Snakes: Life and Language in the Amazonian Jungle.* New York: Pantheon, 2008. Print.

Goleman, Daniel. *Destructive Emotions: How Can We Overcome Them?: A Scientific Dialogue with the Dalai Lama*. New York: Bantam, 2003. Print.

Gyatso, Tenzin. *How to Practice: The Way to a Meaningful Life*. New York: Pocket, 2002. Print.

Hill, Kim, and A. Magdalena. Hurtado. *Aché Life History: The Ecology and Demography of a Foraging People*. New York: Aldine De Gruyter, 1996. Print.

Keltner, D. (2009). *Born To Be Good*. New York: W.W Norton & Company.

Liedloff, J. (1986). *The Continuum Concept*. De Capo Press.

Lekuton, Joseph, and Herman J. Viola. *Facing the Lion: Growing up Maasai on the African Savanna*. Washington, D.C.: National Geographic, 2003. Print.

Miller, G. (2009). *Spent*. New York:Viking Adult

Price, W. (2003). *Nutrition and Physical Degeneration*. Keats.

Ratey, John J., Richard Manning, and David Perlmutter. *Go Wild: Free Your Body and Mind from the Afflictions of Civilization*. Print.

Ricard, Matthieu. *Happiness: A Guide to Developing Life's Most Important Skill*. New York: Little, Brown, 2006. Print.

Ryan, C., & Jetha, C. (2010). *Sex at Dawn*. New York: Harper Collins.

Sisson, Mark. *The Primal Connection*. Malibu, California: Primal Blueprint, 2013. Web.

Schebesta, P. (1938). *Die Bambuti-Pygäen vom Ituri* (Vol. 1). Brussels: Institute Royal Colonial Belge.

Turnball, C. (1987). *Forest People.* Touchstone

Wallace, B. Alan. *The Attention Revolution: Unlocking the Power of the Focused Mind.* Boston: Wisdom Publications, 2006. Print.

Yates, Culadasa John, Matthew Immergut, and Jeremy Graves. *The Mind Illuminated: A Complete Meditation Guide Integrating Buddhist Wisdom and Brain Science.* N.p.: Dharma Treasure, 2015. Print.

Journal Articles

Brewer, J. A., Worhunsky, P. D., Gray, J. R., Tang, Y. Y., Weber, J., & Kober, H. (2011). Meditation experience is associated with differences in default mode network activity and connectivity. *Proceedings of the National Academy of Sciences, 108*(50), 20254-20259.

Buss, D. (2000). The Evolution of Happiness. *American Psychologist* , 15-23.

Carrera-Bastos, P., Fontes-Villalba, M., Lindeberg, S., O'Keefe, J., & Cordain, L. (2011). The western diet and lifestyle and diseases of civilization. *Research Reports in Clinical Cardiology* .

Cordain, Loren, S. Boyd Eaton, Jennie Brand Miller, Staffan Lindeberg, and Clark Jensen. "An Evolutionary Analysis of the Aetiology and Pathogenesis of Juvenile-onset Myopia." *Acta Ophthalmol Scand Acta Ophthalmologica Scandinavica* 80.2 (2002): 125-35. Web.

Cordain, L., Eaton, S. B., Sebastian, A., Mann, N., Watkins, B., O'Keefe, J., et al. (2005). Origins and Evolutions of the Western Diet: Health Implications for the 21st Century. *American Journal of Clinical Nutrition* , 341-355.

Diamond, J. (1993). *The Third Chimpanzee.* New York: Harper Perennial.

Diamond, J. (1987, May). The Worst Mistake in the History of the Human Race. *Discover* .

Diener, E. D. (1996). Most People Are Happy. *Psychological Science , 7.*

Diener, E., & Seligman, M. (2002). Very Happy People. *Psychological Science* , 81-84.

Diener, E., Biswas-Diener, R., & Vitterso, J. (2005). Most people are pretty happy, but there is cultural variation: The Inughuit, the Amish, and the Maasai. *Journal of Happiness Studies* (6), 205-226.

Dolgin, Elie. "The Myopia Boom" *Nature.com.* Nature Publishing Group, 18 Mar. 2015. Web. 27 Apr. 2016.

Finkel, M. (2009, December). *The Hadza.* Retrieved from National Geographic: http://ngm.nationalgeographic.com/2009/12/hadza/finkel-text/1

Frederickson, B. (2009). *Positivity.* New York: Random House.

Fredrickson, B. L., Cohn, M. A., Coffey, K. A., Pek, J., & Finkel, S. M. (2008). Open hearts build lives: positive emotions, induced through loving-kindness meditation, build consequential personal resources. *Journal of personality and social psychology, 95*(5), 1045.

Gibbs, N. (2007). One Day in America. *Time* .

Gray, P. (2009). Play as the Foundation for Hunter-Gatherer Social Existence. *American Journal of Play* , 476-522.

Grinde. (2002). Happiness in the Perspective of Evolutionary Psychology. *Journal of Happiness Studies* , 331-354.

Grinde. (2009). An Evolutionary Perspective on the Importance of Community Relations for Quality of Life. *The Scientific World Journal* .

Grinde, B., & Patil , G. (2009). Biophilia: Does Visual Contact with Nature Impact on Health and Well-Being? *International Journal of Environmental Research and Public Health* , 2332-2343.

Hasenkamp, W., Wilson-Mendenhall, C. D., Duncan, E., & Barsalou, L. W. (2012). Mind wandering and attention during focused meditation: a fine-grained temporal analysis of fluctuating cognitive states. *Neuroimage, 59*(1), 750-760.

Hagerty, M. R., Isaacs, J., Brasington, L., Shupe, L., Fetz, E. E., & Cramer, S. C. (2013). Case study of ecstatic meditation: fMRI and EEG evidence of self-stimulating a reward system. *Neural plasticity, 2013.*

Henricks, J., & Gerard Hall. (2008). The Natural Mysticism of Indigenous Australian Tradition. *Mysticism, Fullness of Life: Homage to Raimon Panikkar.*

Hewlett, B. S., & Hewlett, B. L. (2010). Sex and searching for children among Aka foragers and Ngandu farmers of
Central Africa.

Major, V. (2007). Work time, work interference with family and psychological distress. *Journal of Applied Psychology*
.

Malone, A. (2007, July 20). *Face to face with Stone Age man: The Hadzabe tribe of Tanzania.* Retrieved from The Daily Mail: http://www.dailymail.co.uk/news/article-469847/Face-face-Stone-Age-man-The-Hadzabe-tribe-Tanzania.html

Miller, M. (2003). The Neurobiology and Control of Anxious States. *Progress in Neurobiology* , 83-244.

Lee, R. (1979). *The !Kung San: Men, Women, and Work in a Foraging SocietyThe !Kung San: Men, Women, and Work in a Foraging Society.* New York: Cambridge.

Lee, R., Hansen, J. D., Truswell, A., & Kennelly, B. M. (1972). Blood pressures of !Kung bushmen in Northern Botswana. *American Heart Journal , 84* (1), 5-12.

Noll, R., Shi, K. The last shaman of the Oroqen people of northeast China,*Shaman:Journal of the International Society for Shamanistic Research*17 (1 and 2): 117-140,

Pinker, Steven. "The Brain: The Mystery of Consciousness." *Time.* Time Inc., 29 Jan. 2007. Web. 27 Apr. 2016.

Sikirov, B. A. (1990). Cardio-vascular events at defecation: are they unavoidable?. *Medical hypotheses, 32*(3), 231-233.

Tang, Y. Y., Ma, Y., Wang, J., Fan, Y., Feng, S., Lu, Q., ... & Posner, M. I. (2007). Short-term meditation training improves attention and self-regulation. *Proceedings of the National Academy of Sciences, 104*(43), 17152-17156.

Video

Conscioustv. "Daniel Brown 1 - 'The Great Way' - Interview by Iain McNay." *YouTube*. YouTube, 21 May 2009. Web. 27 Apr. 2016.

GoogleTechTalks. "Shinzen Young: Deep Concentration in Formal Meditation and Daily Life (Theory and Practice)." *YouTube*. YouTube, 24 May 2010. Web. 27 Apr. 2016.

Under21convention07. "Growing Your Face | Dr. Mike Mew | Full Length HD." *YouTube*. YouTube, 18 Mar. 2014. Web. 27 Apr. 2016.